Restorative Solutions
Making it Work

Improving Challenging Behaviour and
Relationships in Schools

Helen Mahaffey and Colin Newton
Published by Inclusive Solutions UK Ltd

Published by Inclusive Solutions UK Limited

April 2008

Design by Chloe Bowles (www.fivebeans.co.uk)

Front Cover Painting by Helen Mahaffey

Printed by Parker & Collinson Ltd

ISBN 0-9546351-4-0

Restorative
Solutions

CONTENTS

ACKNOWLEDGEMENTS

Thanks to Robin Tinker (Nottingham Anti Bullying Support Team Leader) for his extensive work on Restorative Interventions in Nottingham City and elsewhere and for his contributions to this book.

We would like to thank Sir Charles Pollard (ex Chief Superintendent of Thames Valley Police) for his encouragement. Belinda Hopkins (Director Transforming Conflict - the National Centre for Restorative Justice in Educational Settings) for her support and for generously linking us up with contacts around the world.

Many thanks to all the children and their parents and staff in the schools we have worked with; especially those who were part of the Hammersmith and Fulham pilot. By embracing restorative approaches and running with them, they set the stage for restorative practices in schools to unfold in this country and they bring this book alive.

A special appreciation to Janet Clark for her practice, support, warmth and humour all of which made the numerous conferences we have run together a joy.

Thanks to Bethan and Louis Newton plus staff and pupils at Seely Infant School, Nottingham for the artwork throughout the book. Photographs were mainly taken by Colin and Bethan Newton, or organised by Danny and Emerald. Thanks to the range of subjects for agreeing to be included. Thanks to TES for photos on page 78.

Respect and gratitude to Derek Wilson for his patient, detailed editing and substantial support.

Colin would like to thank Elliot, Louis and Bethan Newton for putting up with dad doing his 'psychology thing' on them. Also Jacqui Newton for her unquestioning love and support. Thanks to mum and dad for their unconditional acceptance, inspiration and for being there and just being them.

Helen offers personal acknowledgement to everyone who has been an integral part of her journey through life, both family and friends. A personal thanks especially to her brothers and partner for the love and support they have unfailingly given. Thanks to the many precious nephews, nieces and godchildren who have kept her feet firmly grounded in this area and who have always been a great joy to be around.
'To my mother who has always been a spirited inspiration and my late father who will always be with me in everything I do'.

Thanks also to my colleagues and peers who have helped me remain open and develop my thinking and practice. To Stewart McCafferty who has been a beacon and helped me keep my head in the mountains. I am grateful to Larry Wright for his encouragement and allowing the project to fly and for the attention he has given in the reading of this.'

And for those others, who know who they are....

Bad behaviour in our schools - often leading to school exclusions, speeding the pupils involved to the social scrapheap - has become a blight on our education system. Solutions are hard to come by. Most come in the form of yet more punitive discipline, which merely heightens the problem.

What is needed in schools is fresh thinking, new approaches that work - and Restorative Practices are precisely that. Restorative Practices break the cycle by tackling the root causes of misbehaviour, rather than just massaging the symptoms. Many badly behaved pupils, faced directly and personally with the harm they have done to others, not only see the error of their ways but are often even transformed into positive role models. And they don't need to be excluded.

This book is an invaluable tool for all who want to learn about Restorative Solutions. It describes how, when and where they can be used, not just to reduce exclusions but - even more importantly - to improve the whole behavioural culture of the school and improve attainment. All who work in schools should read it and act on it.

Sir Charles Pollard
Ex Chief Superintendent, Thames Valley Police

FOREWORD

W̲e have been doing this for years without calling it Restorative.

Well, possibly yes, but… Generations of staff in schools have worked imaginatively and hard to resolve conflict and help young people understand how to manage themselves in a demanding world. But in recent years the development of restorative approaches in schools has happened, not because of government initiative, but because practitioners (teachers and support staff) see that the theory and practice of restorative interventions gives a new approach to their work with young people. Staff find that, across a range of interventions from the formal conference to the informal enquiry, restorative interventions are effective in addressing needs and wants of all those involved, holding people to account for their actions, recognising harm caused and laying the foundations for repairing the harm.

The evaluation of Restorative Justice in schools published by the Youth Justice Board in March 2005 gave a real boost to the use of restorative approaches in school demonstrating that of 625 formal Conferences set up, 92% were successful in completing the process and that of those 96% of the agreements made were still in place two to three months after the conference. I know of no comparable effectiveness data for any other intervention.

So why is every school not implementing restorative approaches? I would identify four key areas:

Firstly because this is not something which can be implemented without everyone being engaged with understanding the principles and processes – from Headteacher and Governors through all staff, parents and pupils. This takes time and starts from a rigorous analysis of readiness. This does not mean that everything has to be perfect before a school can start some developments, indeed I found the Trojan Mouse principle (small successes spread the word) was very effective in my school, but there has to be a clear sense of a whole school movement towards being restorative.

Secondly because thorough training is needed, particularly for staff who might undertake the role of facilitator, but also for all staff to have appropriate skills and language to deal with issues restoratively. This range of staff includes the senior leaders of the school as well as the site staff, the reception staff, lunchtime supervisors – and temporary staff – so that everyone is clear that "Restorative interventions is the way we do things here".

Thirdly because schools need to prepare thoroughly for implementing restorative interventions. This ranges from recasting the school behaviour policy, reviewing staff duty procedures, ensuring that the multi agency team working with the school is engaged with any Restorative approach and promoting messages about solving problems to pupils, parents and staff – and more.

Fourthly because it is important to see Restorative approaches being supported by curriculum development. For example schools in England which implement a programme of building social emotional and behavioural skills alongside a restorative approach to resolving conflict are presenting a coherent experience to everyone in the community. Restorative approaches can also be a key source of information for development of the Personal Social and Health Education and Citizenship elements of the curriculum.

So if I were starting to develop Restorative approaches in my school now where would I start?

A Identify support channels for Restorative approaches. In England and Wales your Local Authority or Youth Offending Team may be able to point you to other schools developing restorative approaches.

B Develop an RJ champions team (Staff Pupil Representatives) to drive the process forward perhaps using Chapter Three. These have to have a clear story in their mind about Restorative Approaches and how the school is going to get there (Chapter Five may give help here). Their role is not only planning but building a shared story in the school about how we might 'do things restoratively'.

C Run a training session for Governors of the Pupil Discipline group so they are engaged with the principles and practice.

D Review and change the process for dealing with Fixed Term exclusions to be restorative – particularly the reintegration interview. The aim is to demonstrate to staff that any children returning from Fixed Term exclusion are held to account for their actions, but that their membership of the school community is rebuilt. This way quick wins can be demonstrated to staff.

E Work with School Council on developing further the role of pupils as restorative workers.

Then, progressively, developments can take place towards a whole school restorative approach.

The Restorative approaches movement has come a long way in a very short time. From the innovative leadership of Sir Charles Pollard, past Chief Constable of Thames Valley and leading member of the Youth Justice Board, in developing Restorative Justice within the justice system many professionals in the education field are now customising these approaches to educational settings. The literature for schools on implementing Restorative approaches is still very thin so I am delighted to welcome this important book as a major practical contribution for schools wanting to understand and prepare for implementing restorative approaches.

At a time when much of the discourse in education is rightly about standards and structures it is vital to remind ourselves that effective schools are ones which build relationships for learning. A damaged relationship between child and teacher, between child and child, between child and other adult, or between staff and parents can be a monumental barrier to learning. Restorative approaches which repair relationships, and in doing so give children the skills to manage this for themselves in the future, are a major contribution to school improvement – and also to building the capacity of individuals and communities to be effective in solving problems.

Graham Robb
Secondary Headteacher
Member of Youth Justice Board of England and Wales

'Behold the greatness of acceptance'
Restorative Practices Development Team, University of Waikato, 2003

What are Restorative Solutions all about?

In this chapter we explore:

→ Who this book is aimed at

→ The aims of the book

→ The values that underlie this approach

→ Moving from control to collaboration

→ Shortcomings of Punishment Based Discipline

→ Considering the question of time: weighing up the longer- term costs and advantages of restorative solutions in creating a way forward

→ The long view and the international view

→ Where restorative interventions fit in to work with challenging relationships and behaviour

→ What difference we hope this book will make

→ A view from a head teacher on restorative practices

Restorative Interventions are an exciting and radical approach to dealing with conflict and behaviour that is hard to manage and understand. The approaches are rooted in past traditions and ancient cultures and so there is often a profound sense of returning to solid core values throughout this work.

This book is about Restorative Solutions or Interventions sometimes referred to as Restorative Justice, Restorative Approaches or Restorative Conferencing. At their heart is the idea of 'making it right' - restitution and reparation - not retribution. There will be accounts of these approaches in practice throughout the book.

This is also a book about inclusion. What will it take for us all to just get along? We do not all have to love each other to create a more peaceful place but we do need to find new ways of making accommodations to each other and to talk to each other so that we can co-exist peacefully.

It is also a book about the messy world of relationships and how we can enter into these constructively when things go wrong and people get hurt.
Restorative interventions in schools, educational settings and any environment that includes young people, encourages an understanding, awareness and sensitivity to difference and thereby nurture healthier relationships.

We all exist within complex circles of support, friendship and family in communities of varying connection. In UK society at this time these connections are not always consciously recognised, celebrated or strengthened and we often struggle to find the right words to even communicate with each other about our community membership. Some other cultures appear to have a richer language of their experience of community and connection. For instance in Maori culture whakapapa, for the Navaho hozho and for many Africans the Bantu word ubuntu are used to express these connections. They each recognise that we are all connected in a web of relationships. Reflecting on these cultural differences Howard Zehr commented:

The problem of crime, in this worldview, is that it represents a wound in the community, a tear in the web of relationships. Crime represents damaged relationships. In fact damaged relationships are both a cause and effect of crime. Many traditions have a saying that the harm of one is the harm of all. (Zehr, 2002)

This is a book about the web of relationships and what we need to do when harm occurs between children, between adults, or between children and adults.

We intend to outline exactly what these Restorative Solutions are and how they can be used in all places of learning from the Early Years through to Higher Education. We hope that parents and carers who may be searching for fresh ways to bring up their children will also be able to learn from what is described here.

Who is this book aimed at?

- → School Managers including Headteachers and Principals
- → Class Teachers
- → Special Educational Needs Coordinators
- → Guidance staff
- → Education Welfare Officers
- → Heads of Year
- → Pastoral managers
- → Behaviour support teams
- → Inclusion teams
- → Youth Offending Teams
- → Residential Social Workers and care home staff
- → Social Workers
- → Prevention Teams
- → Youth Inclusion and Support Panels
- → Children's Centre teams
- → Foster and Adoptive Parents
- → Parents and carers

The Aims of this book:

1. To introduce readers to Restorative Solutions and interventions explaining what they are and where they have come from

2. To provide a practical step by step guide to implementing Restorative Interventions in schools and homes

3. To provide a deeper understanding and theoretical, framework for this approach to behaviour, conflict and relationships

Underlying Values Base

When students understand that the goal of discipline is to strengthen them and to teach them, they will no longer be afraid to face their mistakes. They will view a problem as an opportunity for learning in a better way. (Gossen, 2001)

Consider the challenges of relationships in the multiple contexts at play in school life. Add to these children's experiences in their family life and in this community of young people they are members of. Reflect on the challenges faced by children and adults living and working within a wide diversity of culture, race, sexuality, and family make up.

Consider the meaning of the idea of "family" for children who are either in care, separated from parents or siblings, those who have lost family in war or those who are fleeing for survival.

In each of these troubled situations, a restorative mindset would lead us to pose questions such as: What is making this child ill? What makes them truant? What makes them cry? What makes them hurt others? What makes them become violent without a care? A restorative practitioner would have a commitment to a process of restoration and regeneration for all those concerned or involved in a particular episode. Their stance would be non-judgemental, open, curious and neutral.

Any Restorative intervention provides children with the space and opportunity to look at how their own behaviour or words affect another individual and themselves.

We are advocating and striving for a community in which all are included whatever their needs or however challenging their behaviour. The question should no longer be 'should they be here or not?' We now need to ask ' how can we work together to figure out how to meet their needs?'

Relationships are the foundation of a good personalised school, and you cannot build relationships without first cultivating a culture of trust and respect... If kids are going to be respectful, they must feel respected. (Littky, 2002)

From control to collaboration

If we are serious in creating schools and homes where all belong, then we will need to do some serious work to make our organisations, schools, families, care settings and communities much safer. We do not believe this can be achieved through rewards and punishments alone. Both rewards and punishments, says 'Punished by Rewards' author Alfie Kohn (1995), are ways of manipulating behaviour that destroy the potential for real learning. Instead, he advocates providing an engaging curriculum and a caring atmosphere "so kids can act on their natural desire to find out."

Too much time and energy has been spent on rewards and punishments in the past. Today we need more sophisticated, humane approaches that take on board both the individual, the individual in relation to others and the wider systems and relationships in which all operate. For these to be effective, they need to make sense to us and, just as importantly, to the children and young people in our care whom we are trying to educate. We need to listen to children and young people, so that they can tell us what they would like to happen in times of conflict.

Controlling others is ultimately an impossible task, and we often seriously compromised our ethics and basic respect by trying. Any success that depends on the compliance of others inevitably will be frustrating and inspire resentment. (Lovett, 1996)

Has excluding pupils proved an effective sanction? The figures and facts in the box opposite would certainly cause any reader to question this.

'Almost 10% of 13 and 14-year-old boys were suspended in 2005 because of poor behaviour, official figures show. More than 200,000 pupils of all ages were given a total of 344,000 fixed-term exclusions, according to the first comprehensive set of figures on temporary exclusions published by the Department for Education and Skills. The figures also reveal that the numbers of pupils permanently excluded had risen sharply to its highest level since 2000. There were 9,880 permanent exclusions in 2003-4, a 6% increase on the previous year, despite increased use of in-school units for disruptive pupils'.
(TES, 1 July 2005)

Some Exclusion Facts

Around 10,000 pupils are permanently excluded from school each year. The number of permanent exclusions has remained broadly unchanged over the last five years, despite falling sharply in the late 1990s. The rate of permanent exclusion is much lower in Scotland than elsewhere: 4 per 10,000 pupils each year compared to more than 12 in England and 10 in Wales. Despite substantial reductions in recent years, Black Caribbean pupils are still three times as likely to be excluded from school as White pupils.

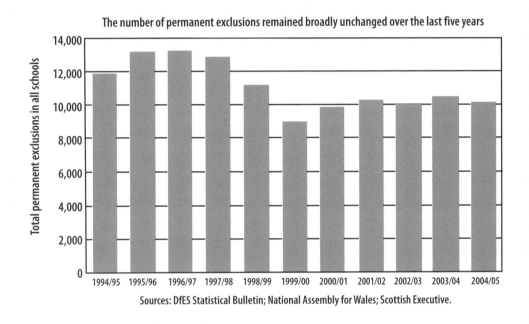

The number of permanent exclusions remained broadly unchanged over the last five years

Sources: DfES Statistical Bulletin; National Assembly for Wales; Scottish Executive.

It is nearly 20 years since corporal punishment was banned in schools, although caning continued legally in Public schools until the late nineties.

As we (the authors) started this book, OFSTED announced their concern about declining behaviour in secondary schools and noted improving behaviour in primary schools over the last 3 years (OFSTED, February, 2005). Many would argue that much more radical approaches to behaviour and emotions are needed in secondary schools (See for instance the work of Dennis Littky, 2002). There is a need for particular attention to be paid to relationships as a priority over academic subjects as the main work of every teacher. We would love to see 'friendship' as the top priority of all curriculum activity. We certainly agree with Belinda Hopkins (2003) that there is less of a need for 'Behaviour' policies and a much greater need for a 'Relationship' policy in every school (Thorsbourne, 2002).

We believe in creating mainstream schools where all belong; where the answer to the question; who would you include is simply: All means all. Imagine what could be created by diverting our energies and resources away from the special, the separate, the expert, the stand-alone, the segregated? A shift towards true partnerships, relational and person/ people focused, respectful and flexible teams that can do what it takes in local mainstream community settings would make inclusion a reality.

Exploring multiple perspectives around victim's needs and offender's needs

One very interesting exercise, which we have found to be effective and thought provoking amongst many groups of colleagues, is to conduct a "Needs" audit for both victims and offenders.

Asking the questions (Blood, 2000):

"What do you need when you have been harmed or hurt?"

and

"What do you need when you have harmed or hurt someone?"

will generate a long list of answers, the vast majority of which will reflect "restorative" needs.

Reflect on your own answer to these questions.

Another exercise to elicit strengths and abilities is to conduct a much wider audit across the whole school community about what has proved most effective from a personal experience at times of conflict or difficult relationships with peers. We have found that a simple set of questions around this has brought forth many untapped restorative capacities. These often go unnoticed and may be invisible around a school when indeed, there may be pupils especially who bring a whole range of skills such as mediation and peer support which could be utilized and developed, into a restorative resource pool.

Shortcomings of Punishment Based Discipline

When a teacher responds to incidents and events around school, which need a disciplinary reaction, that adult has to make a number of on the spot judgements. Many adults will use a broadly Restorative approach but, too often, challenging behaviour is dealt with in a punitive way.

Punishment does not usually meet the needs of those who suffered as a result of the incident. Typically, sanctions focus on the person who has caused the harm and not on the person on the receiving end of the harmful actions. Those who suffered often do not get a meaningful apology, or any explanation of what happened, or why they were singled out. They may fear a reoccurrence as soon as the "offending" pupil returns to the school or the classroom, or they may harbour a sense of somehow being responsible for what happened. Because of this, the incident is often left unresolved for those who have been harmed.

When we look at the needs of those who have in some way been harmed, those most often expressed by teachers and other adult practitioners include:

Someone to listen to me and support me.

Reassurance that it won't happen again.

A sincere, genuine apology (maybe in private).

The answer to "why me?"

Time to get over it and calm down.

Some kind of justice.

When schools use the traditional, punitive approach to misbehaviour, these needs are rarely met. In terms of the child or young person who has harmed or offended another child, the punitive or retributive approach is often based on the theory of deterrence. In practice, however, punishment does not always work as a deterrent. It may be that:

There is some perceived "street cred" attached to punishment.

Children and young people who have caused harm to others do not have to face the full effects of their actions and may delude themselves that any harm they did was not important.

If the person being punished feels isolated, it may be more difficult for them to get back into the school community, thus making it more attractive to break the rules.

If the problem behaviour does persist, the young person may be pushed down a road of exclusion and marginalisation. They may be excluded from the school but remain a problem in the wider community.

So when we ask, "What do you need when you have harmed someone?" respondents most often give the following answers:

Forgiveness.

A new start or a clean slate.

A chance to make amends or put things right.

A chance to apologise.

A chance to explain why.

Closure – an assurance it won't be brought up again.

Adults working in education rarely feel that they themselves need punishment, isolation, exclusion or special placement!

When a school uses a traditional punitive approach to misbehaviour, these underlying needs are rarely met.

Asking any group to consider which of these needs are met by "traditional" school punishments such as detention, isolation from the peer group or exclusion will lead to the inevitable conclusion that neither the needs of the child who has been harmed nor the child who was responsible for the harm are met by such punishments. We are suggesting that the range of skills and practices within a restorative framework offers a wide set of tools which are effective in addressing a variety of difficult behaviours and relationship issues.

How do people, especially young people, feel if their needs are not met?

Transferring this thought to a typical incident in a school can also be very thought provoking:

JOHN AND PETER

John snatches Peter's pencil case when teacher isn't looking and empties it on to the floor. Peter tells the teacher. Peter is upset because two pencils have broken. At the next opportunity an adult speaks to John and Peter.

Adult:	"I want to speak to both of you now"
	"I saw what happened, John. You took Peter's pencil case and threw it on to the floor". *(John interrupts)* "I'm speaking, I don't want to hear that. John, you are losing your playtime today to stay in with me and help me clean the paint pots and you will apologise to Peter now".
John:	*Says nothing*
Adult:	"We're waiting, John"
John:	*(Quietly)* "Sorry"
Adult:	"I'm really disappointed with you, John. You are always being naughty in lessons. Go back to your seat and get on with your work". *John stamps off, obviously angry.*
Adult:	*(To Peter)* "OK, Peter, that's sorted that out, pick up your pencils and go back to your seat and try and get on with John". *Peter tries to say something but adult interrupts.* "I've sorted it, Peter. Off you go". *Peter walks off slowly, looking worried and disappointed.*

Some questions to consider

What did you think of John's apology?

What did you think of the punishment John was given?

What did you think about telling John he's "always naughty"?

How does John feel?

What did you think of the way Peter and his feelings were handled?

How does the adult feel?

Did John or Peter have their needs met?

Was the relationship repaired?

Would you agree?

1) That the incident described is very typical of the low-level behaviour which happens every day in most UK schools at Key Stage 2 or even Key stage 3, and

2) That the way the adult deals with the incident is often the default way that such an incident is handled.
("What happened?" "Who is to blame?" "What punishment is appropriate?")

It is important to stress that we are not making judgements about the way the adult has handled this situation. We recognise that pressures of time and expectation often mean that busy teachers and support staff respond in this way. Many colleagues will handle this incident in this way, because as far as they are concerned, "it works". By unpicking the incident it becomes clear that neither John nor Peter will have had many, if any, of their needs met. It is useful at this point to refer back to the "Needs" list that we considered earlier. If needs are not being met by this type of punishment, why do some/many schools persist in working in this way and what will the long term consequences be?

"John and Peter" can provide a glimpse of an answer to the often-asked question "But when will I have TIME to do all this?" Most education professionals will recognise that in this story it is possible that John will exact his own retribution on Peter at playtime or lunchtime, and that a much more serious situation will have to be resolved, causing many more people much more work.

Considering the question of time:

Weighing up the longer - term costs and advantages of restorative solutions in creating a way forward

There can be times that a large group or groups of young people may have become involved, in varying degrees, in conflicts that span over different periods of time. In these cases pockets of individuals may be directly involved in conflict with each other at a particular point and the rest of their group by association will join in. A process of layering may then occur.

One young person described being involved in such a conflict as being "like a snowball rolling down a hill with no way of getting out" another described the process as; "the whole thing getting bigger and more serious with people getting really hurt as a result". We have often heard children and young people involved in such a conflict saying that they are "not really sure why" they are involved in the conflict or why it is that they don't get on with the other young people or what the conflict is really about. We have heard how these young people also feel "unsafe" about what "could" happen but at the same time not really knowing what to do. One young person described always having to look over her shoulder whilst walking down the school corridors.

BEEF RAP

One day at school, all going well
And next day things changed and god it was hell!

We'd had a cross word, then sucking of teeth
And all very quickly it turned into "big beef"

"Go on go on fight her don't worry you'll win"
Everyone circled as we got "stuck in"

The cuts and the bruises for them they will cure
But watching over my shoulder each moment....I'm not so sure

Every day it gets worse, I'm feeling so tense
Why did it happen? It don't make no sense

And then we had this meeting where we all had our say
We talked in a circle...You know, it was ok

I'm not saying it's easy cause you're both feeling rough
But in talking it through it gets less and less tough

She said she felt angry and wished I was dead
I realised I'd offended her in what I had said

It felt in that meeting we'd got to the core
And by talking together we settled the score

So whatever your "beef" or what troubles you bring
Just sit down together and do that talking thing

Sophie

Case Study: "Sorting things out together"

When restorative interventions were being pioneered in secondary schools in London, little was known about these practices and how they would translate to a school setting. One of the first restorative justice referrals made to a new project in one secondary school was initially described by the referrer as a "girl gang" incident, a fight that had occurred in the corridor during one of the breaks.

There were various staff accounts and descriptions around the episode and in relation to what had been emerging and escalating over a period of nearly two years between two groups of year nine and ten girls. The sense was that, for some of the teaching staff who had to manage the various scuffles in class, they had lost sight of the individual pupils within a homogeneous whole. Some described a "wave" of intimidation "sweeping" the school and this along with the belief that it was becoming out of control concerned them.

Words like "gang culture" were creeping into some of the descriptions and to some extent became a self fulfilling prophecy for some of the girls in the group who acted into these descriptions in varying degrees.

Most members of staff were concerned especially about the effects of the levels of disruption in and around the school and upon those pupils who were directly affected by being in the same class.

From an independent restorative position, we quickly realised that the identified incidents occurred within a particular context of "derogatory comments" and disdainful "looks", and that, there was an intricate history to the relationships between the individuals in the group. Indeed, for some of the girls, this dated back to primary school.

At the Head Teacher's large conference table, the two groups of girls, fifteen of them in total, awaited their "punishment". They expected another exclusion to go with the many they had accrued for smaller incidents in the past. "We are going to try something different a restorative conference" the Head uttered, whilst reminding them that there were a set of school rules which they had breached. This was actually a crucial point. The head was able to take a risk, suspend disbelief and try out a new approach. The fact that this was new meant no one really knew what this approach would look like in action and therefore there were some misconceptions for the girls and indeed some staff at this stage. For example most of the girls thought they had no choice but to participate in a restorative conference thinking that if they chose not to they would be facing lengthy exclusions. One of the first points highlighted for them was that their participation in the restorative conference was a choice and not and ultimatum.

By introducing the voluntary nature of attending a restorative conference, a stark difference was experienced by all the girls. One by one, they were asked for their consent to participate in the process. Asked what they needed to coexist in the school, overwhelmingly they said "to sort things out", as it was getting in the way of their learning and was something that all their parents were concerned about.

This set a more constructive context in which to proceed. We will be detailing an example of next stage of a restorative conference further in the book. The overall process did take TIME (two weeks time in total) with each group being seen separately, then each pupil individually, followed by a set of one to one conferences and bringing the large group together again to share the agreements they had made at the end. A meeting with parents and staff involved with the girls at that stage acknowledged what the girls had achieved and, importantly, enlisted them as ongoing support to help each individual keep to their agreements.

The long-term benefits were of huge value and highly effective with no ongoing disputes or conflict resulting. Whilst there were initial observations by some members of staff that this was a lengthy process, it was considered, overwhelmingly, to have been worth the time and effort. This conference launched "Restorative Justice" practices in this particular school and their new logo "Sorting things out together" summed up the essence of the approach.

The long view and the international view

New ways of thinking about behaviour and relationships with children and young people can pave the way in the longer term towards a more peaceful world. Our young people need new ways of relating to each other, new ways of making accommodations to the challenges that human relationships pose and, most of all, new ways of handling conflicts that do not lead to escalation, punitive approaches, bullying or violence. In a world of conflict young people may have profound experiences of extreme violence, sometimes directly or indirectly and we cannot assume what life is like for a young person whose family has had to flee their country due to war and has experienced multiple loss and displacement.

Where do Restorative Interventions fit in?

The following list is a possible sequence for the development of pupil involvement in peer support and restorative approaches. We have found that full-blown formalised restorative justice conferences, as discussed in subsequent chapters, are best reserved for the most complex or most serious situations those that would typically lead to exclusion processes. Each named approach is more or less restorative and each recognises the importance of direct pupil involvement in bringing about change. Our dream would be that restorative interventions could ultimately replace exclusions as the school's response to rule breaking.

This model provides a range of options to meet the many needs and demands of children, young people and their families as well as the needs and demands of school and community settings.

Circle time

Whole group of young people in a class or tutor group discuss behaviour/emotional issues together on regular basis.
When to use? Daily meeting of group

School Council

Group of marginalised high profile pupils involved in decision making about running of school.
When to use? Half termly strategic meeting regarding school's policy on Behaviour and Attendance

Playground Friends / Friendship benches

Playgrounds divided into zones where everyone encouraged to help/ befriend each other.

When to use? All Playtimes/Breaktimes/Lunchtimes

Peer Tutoring (academic work)

The matching of pupils in class settings to support achievement in specific subject areas.

When to use? Set times of week with targeted groups/individuals around curriculum area such as reading/PSHE

"Buddies" (1-1 befriending)

Sharing time and giving 1-1 support regularly. Target group (or "little buddies") are often vulnerable children.

When to use? New pupils joining school with difficult history or transition points

Peer Mediation

Non violent conflict resolution.

When to use? Trained team of pupils to be on duty daily at breaktimes/lunchtimes

Peer Mentoring (combats disaffection or loneliness)

Helping to explore and sometimes solve problems by giving positive feedback and the benefit of experience.

When to use? Focused use with targeted pupils at transition times

Circles of Friends

Focused inclusive involvement of peers, enables members of a class or peer group to give time and thought to how they can be supportive towards a fellow pupil in the things they do and let him know that they care about who and how he is.

When to use? With high profile challenging or highly vulnerable pupils at risk of exclusion or segregation

Peer Counselling

A confidential listening service focused on a particular issue such as bullying.
When to use? Whole school strategy to combat bullying

Restorative Conferencing

Pupils involved in restorative justice style conferencing.
When to use? Alternative to fixed/permanent exclusions, high profile incidents of rule breaking where there is a clear victim and offender

We all have the power to listen to voices that are seldom heard. If we choose to make the time, to learn to listen and to struggle with the pain and frustration that disempowered people feel, we will see new visions, feel new energy, and find hope in our future. There is power in the powerless. We can be catalysts, or encrusted residue. The choice is ours. (Pearpoint, 1993)

What difference will this book make?

It's the difference that will make the difference" (Bateson 1972)

How can this way of working make a real difference to schools and other settings? Our experience is that the successful use of this resource will contribute to the following:

→ Increased use of restorative approaches in schools and care situations.

→ Pupils will feel more listened to.

→ Conflicts will be dealt with more peacefully and effectively.

→ Exclusions will reduce.

→ Headteachers, SENCOS, teachers and teaching assistants and a wide range of educational staff will have learned some new processes to change pupil behaviour, reduce conflicts and improve school ethos.

→ More pupils with the most challenging emotional needs will be effectively included in local mainstream school settings.

Yet while there is widespread acceptance in principle of the reasons for increasing inclusion, the fundamental changes in practice that will be needed to bring this about are much slower to appear. Inclusion doesn't just happen, and if we are serious about these values then, we will need to do something differently, adopting new tools and approaches, and doing the hard work to see them through. (Newton and Wilson, Circles of Friends, 2003)

A view from a head teacher on restorative practices

Commenting on the introduction of what was at the time a very different and new approach in schools in the London Borough of Hammersmith and Fulham one head teacher described the Restorative Justice in Schools Project as:

"One of the most successful projects we've got in terms of behaviour strategies. We have integrated the principle of reparation and restoration into our disciplinary policy".

 She went on to say that:

"… taking responsibility for what went wrong and doing something to put it right has now become part of our culture".

(Passmore, Times Educational Supplement 2003)

CHAPTER 2
Definitions and Background

'He that spareth his rod hateth his son'

Proverbs

In this chapter we will examine:

→ What Restorative Solutions can provide in a school context

→ Why Restorative Solutions now?

→ Punishment and Control or a Community of Care?

→ Making Collaboration a Reality

→ The historical background to this way of approaching conflicts and rule breaking 20th Century Revival of Restorative Justice

→ Criminal Justice background of Restorative Justice in the United Kingdom

→ The Promise of Restorative Interventions

→ Definitions, vocabulary and some of the key concepts that have emerged within the restorative field

→ The restorative approach and the methods it encompasses

→ Practice principles

→ Developing a relationship policy

→ A restorative school where everyone benefits

What can Restorative Solutions provide in a school context?

Why is that important now?

At times, both inside and out of the school setting, there are extreme and tragic consequences of not dealing with peer relationships, conflict, raised tensions and issues of bullying and intimidation of some young people towards their peers and others. Sadly, a number of these cases have ended in a child being killed or taking their own life and these have been well documented in the media.

We are presented with a serious challenge and questions about what we can do to make the difference for young people. We want them to feel safe and enabled to resolve, what are for them, some very complex issues at various stages of their development, and to ensure safety within the school and outside the school gates.

This is not solely about policy and strategy. This is about a practical, embodied response to a range of behaviours pupils exhibit to each other.

Much of this is about what we do in these situations and the potential value and benefit in terms of moving things on constructively whilst maintaining everyone's dignity. It is about getting in before it is too late to intervene.

Punishment and Control or Community of Care?

Punishment and control simply do not work. Their impact is limited in terms of changing undesired behaviours, addressing conflict in complex relationships or in creating a more harmonious, collaborative environment.

Retribution is a familiar concept in relation to punishment, encapsulated in such sayings as 'an eye for an eye' and 'getting their just desserts'. Sentences are arrived at according to the relevant categories of offence, and in relation to other, similar cases, so that fairness is assured, and justice is seen to be done. Offences are deemed to be offences against the state, and it is the state that is responsible for sentencing and punishment, according to law. (Drewery, 2004)

In contrast, restorative solutions focus on the social and emotional impact of offences and are:

...preoccupied with processes that will not only redress the effect of the offence on the victim, but will also restore the situation, including the damage done to relationships, and even to offenders themselves. In this paradigm, wrongdoing is seen as primarily a violation of people and of relationships. The focus is on the harmful effects of offending. Offenders are required to meet those affected, to take responsibility for their actions, and to make amends. A major feature of the approach is that it brings together a community of care around both the offender and those affected, and both 'sides' share in the resolution of the problem. (Drewery, 2004)

The failure of retributive systems of behaviour management in schools in the UK and beyond is all too obvious. As we write, in the UK permanent exclusions and non-attendance figures continue to rise and increasing numbers of young people are placed in Learning Support Units and Pupil Referral Units. Whilst the intention might be to mobilise resources and focus intensive support where needed, these are usually very temporary measures. In effect, we are stripping young people of longer-term resources at a time when they most need them. Money spent on short term special settings might well be better invested in longer term mainstream school systemic changes. From our experience, it is precisely the young people who are: disenfranchised, disillusioned and usually termed "disruptive", who are also resource hungry. Moving them out of mainstream settings simply increases the likelihood of reduced achievement, lowered self esteem, further offending and long term dislocation from communities.

We need another way. I have been teaching for 30 years and have been a head for 10. I cannot keep excluding pupils from the local estate, I am just feeding the local crime figures as I push these pupils back on to the streets and doing nothing for the next generation. (Comment in a training session: Scottish Headteacher, 2004)

Are Restorative Solutions that other way?
What openings can a restorative perspective offer?
What does restoration mean for a community or school?

Take a moment to think about your school.

Think about the incidents and behaviours that are inappropriate or very difficult to manage. These may range from sexualised behaviour, bullying and fire setting.

How would you describe your school's response to these or other difficult behaviours and incidents that may occur?

How would you describe your personal response to these?

How effective do you feel these processes are:

→ In reducing the likelihood of further incidents

→ In helping young people learn how to get along more successfully with others?

→ In promoting Citizenship values?

Making collaboration a reality

Restorative working typically invites collaboration between those harmed and those who have harmed along with other key stakeholders. Teachers and other adults are invited to collaborate with those they may find difficult to work with, or even to like.

Herb Lovett in his work with some of the most 'difficult' adults in the US concludes that we must move away from control and embrace collaboration.

It is in listening to people with difficult behaviour that positive approaches contrast most clearly with current traditions of service. In the world of positive approaches, we work in collaboration and in a spirit of openness, honesty and equality. (Learning to Listen, Lovett 1996)

Positive approaches would include those that are restorative at heart.

Talking and doing "to" tends to easily become punitive, which too often has the effect of stigmatising those involved.

Talking and doing "with", on the other hand, operates within a restorative frame, is collaborative and it can have the effect of being re-integrative and positive in impact.

The wider historical context of Restorative "Justice"

It may be helpful to look at where these ideas originated and how they have gathered momentum and become organised in the UK. This may then provide some insight as to how Restorative approaches and practices may be best organised in your setting. The historical context provides us with the foundations of what has become a wide-ranging field.

Restorative Justice is far from being a new school of thought and has its roots in the traditions of justice of the ancient Arab, Greek and Roman civilizations. For the ancient Indian Hindus "he who atones is forgiven". (Van Ness, 1986).

Indeed, restorative justice was the dominant model across much of Europe until the Norman Conquest. Then there was a shift to a position where crime was seen as a matter of felony against the king rather than a wrong done to another person. (Braithwaite 1999). This meant that any crime became a crime against the state requiring the state to "punish" the "offender". The needs of those who had been harmed therefore were forgotten.

20th Century Revival of Restorative Justice

New Zealand introduced conferencing in 1989 as part of the Children and Families Act of that year. Taking the lead from the Maori commitment to community–based, culturally appropriate solutions to offending and individual or group conflicts, it marked a radical shift in the whole system's approach to criminal and social welfare matters.

The Maori saw an offence as a sign of failure for a family, and the wider community, not just of the individual offender, and they wanted much greater involvement in the decision making process. (Hopkins, 2004)

Detention centres were closed and responses to offending changed. This was a bold experiment. It deprofessionalised the process of dealing with children and youth and empowered families to take greater responsibility for their own children. It has since influenced philosophy and practice in the fields of social work and criminal justice worldwide.

The idea of "scripting" for a conference was introduced two years later in Wagga Wagga, New South Wales, Australia in 1991. It was adapted for use by community police officers to help them move into a distinctively different role in conferences, and to generally aid them facilitating conferences. It also simplified the process of conducting conferences and helped ensure a more reliable result.

It is fascinating to track the cultural and historical twists and turns that have led to an interest in RJ in the UK. Just over 100 years ago the Maori were viewed and dealt with much less respectfully than today. Ironically we are now trying to learn from the early Maori traditions of restorative process.

Thinking of an interpretive metaphor for this historical scene I am trying to paint, I can think of no more potent image than that of King Tawhiao, a Maori king who in the late nineteenth century led a group by ship to England to petition Queen Victoria about grievances concerning what they saw as breaches of the Treaty. I imagine Tawhiao, dressed according to English protocol in morning suit and tails, cutting a fine figure with his facial moko and feather in his hair. Victoria's officials refused them permission to see her (Orange, 1987). While Maori have continued to interrogate and in many cases embrace the mores of the Pakeha, at the same time, in spite of assimilationist policies early in the twentieth century, they have never ceded their own sovereignty, including their rights to their own cultural values. Education is one of the discursive grounds upon which this struggle continues. During the early twentieth century for example, many Maori children were caned for talking Maori at school, even though they may not have spoken any English before they got to school (Edwards, 1990). And some of these women and men are the grandparents and great grandparents of children who are now being suspended from schools. (Drewery, 2004)

Criminal Justice background of Restorative Justice in the United Kingdom

Criminal Justice in the UK has traditionally required the state to determine blame or guilt and imposed appropriate punishment, reflecting the requirement that offenders get what they deserve and that if punished sufficiently will be less likely to repeat the crime. Criminal Justice focuses on:

- ⟶ What laws have been broken?
- ⟶ Who did it?
- ⟶ What punishment do they deserve?

RJ contrasts, focusing on:

- ⟶ What happened?
- ⟶ Who has been hurt?
- ⟶ What are their needs?

RJ has emerged as a significant feature of our justice system over the last two decades. Its prominence was marked by its appearance in the Youth Justice and Criminal Evidence Act 1999 reflecting a significant shift in governmental thinking.

Thames Valley Police have played a key part in promoting restorative practices in the UK and have no doubt influenced the government's strategy to mainstream restorative justice. Restorative cautioning was creatively adopted by Thames Valley and restorative methods were integrated into police and preventative work including schools and elsewhere. Policy makers have been particularly attracted to these new ideas to improve "victim" support and services. Restorative cautioning and conferencing were piloted in Aylesbury in 1997 and have operated in all of the eleven Thames Valley Police areas since 1998 for adults as well as young people. The evaluation of these restorative approaches and methods as a way of dealing with young and persistent offenders found very high levels of satisfaction by everyone involved. (Tickell and Akester 2004)

Police conferences were introduced not only to encourage young people to take responsibility for their actions but also to improve what were perceived to be the deteriorating relationships between police and young people. Underpinning this has been the theory of re-integrative shaming (Braithwaite 1989) that purports that society's support for wrongdoers as people, combined with disapproval of their behaviour, is effective in reducing offending. The intention of the key questions is to raise issues of responsibility, reparation and reintegration.

We provide detailed evaluation information in Chapter 8 but it is worth noting here that an independent evaluation in 2002 found that young offenders aged 10 to 17 who were party to a restorative approach (via a restorative caution) were only half as likely to be re-sanctioned within a year.

The Promise of Restorative Interventions in Schools

Promotes Inclusion - for all involved. "Victims" have a voice and stake in the process and "perpetrators" are held to account and given an opportunity to do something, which will help the situation and mend the relationship. Restoration provides an opportunity to remain, to continue to belong, as opposed to being excluded or removed to a more 'special' setting.

Encourages Responsibility - for those who cause harm by acknowledging and "facing" the person who has been on the receiving end of their actions. Here, whether directly or indirectly, "the other" becomes a person with thoughts and feelings within a network of others who also may have been affected in some way. It therefore puts the humanity back into the equation.

Provides an Effective Intervention - in stopping or deterring undesired behaviour on a long-term basis. This stuff is powerful and can actually work. It impacts on the complex and messy world of relationships, which are at the heart of so many conflicts. The approach encourages the rule breaker to focus on the direct effects and the ripple effects of their behaviour on others.

RJ processes can be used in situations where the relationship between a pupil and member of staff has broken down.

Examples of this and other complex scenarios will be detailed later along with possible restorative strategies and responses. The promise is that schools will have at their disposal a range of restorative interventions to fit the need of the situation, the needs of the pupils/young people involved and the wider needs of the organisation.

Supports Behaviour Improvement Policies and Citizenship teaching

- As we write this book the development of citizenship is growing in significance within the school curriculum. RJ can help to turn the somewhat abstract ideas of citizenship and democracy in schools into reality. The Advisory Group on Education for Citizenship and the Teaching of Democracy in Schools have encouraged schools to promote:

"Skills and values relevant to the nature and practices of participative democracy; the duties, responsibilities, rights and development of pupils into citizens; and the value to individuals, schools and society of involvement in the local and wider community" (DfES strategy 2006)

RJ fits within the key objectives in the DfES strategy 2006 to:

"…enable all young people to develop and to equip themselves with the skills, knowledge and personal qualities needed for life and work"

RJ, has the potential to contribute significantly to both the achievement of the DfES's wider aims of creating a safer school community, and to specific targets in this area.

Restorative Justice has been piloted and rolled out nationally in a number of schools across the UK with the aims of reducing school exclusions, increasing attendance and addressing issues of bullying. By using more restorative approaches, methods and techniques to address difficult behaviours, young people, it is hoped, will get a consistent message of taking responsibility for their actions and making amends. This can become part of a whole school approach to help maintain them in school and the community.

Addressing Bullying Restoratively

- Bullying in schools has, at times, been responded to by a more organised takeover by stronger groups of young people, whose movements become more coordinated. Many younger and more vulnerable young people may be attracted to the membership of these groups and may find themselves being victimised within the "pecking order". There may be a great number of innocent young people, either playing in the playground or outside the school gates, who cannot escape some of the deadly weapons that are being used, sometimes, sadly, with fatal consequences.

Bullying is of course a very complex topic and one to which we will be giving more detailed attention to later in this book. We cannot however underestimate the direct impact of international conflicts such as events in Iraq, and personal conflicts and relationships as portrayed through the media upon our children and young people in their day-to-day relations with each other.

Bullying: Some Questions for Self Reflection

If we were to view bullying behaviour as a child communicating something to you, what would the child be saying? What would their needs be?

More personally and more uncomfortably: where would you place yourself and other adults around you on the spectrum of behaviours that get described as "bullying"?

These would include those which you may have been party to? The spectrum may range from name calling, spreading rumours, insensitivity towards others and misusing one's power through to verbal and physical assault.

Supports the development of a Relationship Policy - Restorative Solutions can and are forming part of many school's sanctions and behaviour policy. In fact, it is leading to many schools adopting a new and much more dynamic 'relationships' policy, featuring such fine but long ignored concepts as 'forgiveness'. So it's out with the Behaviour Policy and in with a much fuller Relationships policy.

The process of RJ is about enabling informed and thoughtful responses highlighting the importance of rights and responsibilities. It promotes what we could call relational responsibility, which is about people relating to each other as social moral beings with rights and duties plus responsibilities. RJ actions a respect for diversity and difference and, therefore, promotes cultural awareness and sensitivity. It encourages pupils to become self reflective and more responsive and responsible within the school environment, the community and society as a whole.

A Restorative School

What might a Restorative School Policy look like?
Restorative solutions are characterised by responding to and accepting the challenge of new ways of educating children and young people.

According to 'The Restorative Practices Development Team', New Zealand 2003, a restorative school:

Bravely takes on a new look at a traditional process of educating.

The centrality of judgement, deficit and failure is displaced by appreciation, alternative possibilities and hope.

Issues are addressed rather than students punished.

Teachers see themselves as being in an equal relationship with students and their parents, not as authorities over them.

When disciplinary offences occur, the focus is on restoring order through restoring the relationship rather than restoring authority.

The 'mana' of individual students is maintained and grown and not diminished.

The school community is committed to the integrity of all its members.

People speak respectfully of one another, including teachers, students and their families, recognising that all families want success for their children.

Teachers and students look forward to the challenges they meet in school.

The voice of every student is heard rather than drowned out by the loudest or weightiest.

Excellence is sought in respectful relationships.

Ensuring that everyone belongs in a school community is valued more than offering privileges to the few.

Hospitality is extended to parents and visitors.

The communities of care around the school and its students become very visible.

Students learn that living in a complex community is not only possible, it also can be enjoyable.

There are significantly fewer referrals to the office for bad behaviour.

School achievement soars.

Peace breaks out.

We remember what we are here for.

Mana

A more complex notion of community identity, linked to self-esteem and self-respect, is known by the Maori as "mana".

Maori have a concept, mana, that is something like agency, but it is also more than that. Mana includes a sense of strength, and respect. It is what is honoured about a person, and it is one of the aspects of a person that can grow, or be diminished.

The mana of a person is tied inextricably to the mana of their tribe and family, and vice versa. Maori protocols hold as explicit that no-one should have their mana diminished by a process of coming together for redress. Indeed, the mana of a tribe or family is increased when someone who has given offence, or their tribe or family, does what is necessary to offer redress. This is quite a different psychology from the individualized idea that an offender must be diminished or shamed before they can be built back up. (Drewery, 2004)

Definitions, Vocabulary and Key Concepts

Restorative Solutions

Martin Luther King, drawing upon his experience of challenging racism in the US, taught us that we could love a person whilst hating their actions (King, 1963). The separation of person and actions are at the heart of restorative solutions to wrongdoing. The restorative approach supports the "value" and "intrinsic worth" of the wrongdoer whilst directly addressing his or her actions (Watchel, 1999).

Methods which are Restorative

Restorative interventions include:

- Empathic listening
- Circle Time
- Restorative Conferencing
- Restorative discussions and enquiries
- Mediation
- Restorative Circles
- Circles of Friends
- Family Conferencing
- Victim Empathy
- Restorative Justice

We use the term Restorative Justice (RJ) to reflect the formal conferencing end of this continuum of approaches to intervening with broken relationships and offending.

The Restorative Conference is an attractive option for:

→ *'Schools who are wanting to do something more constructive than continually punish, and eventually exclude or expel troublesome young people;*

→ *Victims of incidents, who can have a greater say in the process of setting things to rights;*

→ *Those who fall foul of school authorities and their families, who without a similar process may be left frustrated and angry at the system that seems to abandon their educational needs.'* (Drewery, 2004)

A useful starting point in thinking about the place that restorative interventions may currently occupy in your school or residential setting may be to reflect on any restorative practice that is currently occurring.

What is Restorative Justice?

We are using the term RJ to represent the formal conferencing element which is placed at one end of a continuum of restorative solutions that ranges from restorative listening, mediation, circle time, through processes such as circles of friends and restorative discussions or conversations to more formal conferences. One of the key aims within the restorative process is to reconnect people when relationships for whatever reason have broken down. We need to transform relationships not just adopt a nice approach to discipline as Wendy Drewery so well argues in our Afterword.

At the centre of the idea of restoration is relationship
(Drewery, Winslade, McMenamin 2002)

Restorative Solutions and Restorative Justice sit at the formal end of an approach or philosophy, which has at its centre a set of core principles. These can be applied in different ways and in different settings.

Core Restorative Principles

There is a need for individuals who have harmed to take responsibility for their actions and the affect of these on others

There are consequences to the person they have harmed, (these may be physical/emotional/practical) and possibly to others indirectly affected

Things can be restored and repaired

Inclusion is always the starting point

Communication - all parties are in a "dialogical space" (Bakhtin, 1986), where everyone's sense of agency is respected within an ethical framework so as to unpack some of the complexities of what has occurred and to facilitate a more constructive way forward

Empowerment – of all parties, "a win/win"

Moving on positively and creating new relationships based on respect for the individual

Practice Principles

The focus initially is on what has happened, hearing from all parties equally

There is something in the process, which benefits everyone

There is a focus on the effect of actions and or words. This includes not just the person who is directly affected but parents, carers, siblings, peers and whoever else has been impacted upon

Significant others are actively involved in working towards a solution/resolution (directly if it is a conference involving parents/carers, and indirectly if others can help pupil to keep to contract)

There is a move towards making some kind of agreement or contract, which comes from the pupils themselves and in their own words. These are based on the wishes of the person who has been wronged and take into account how things can be done differently in the future

Safety – it (a conference) is set up in a way that everyone will know and feel safe with the structure, confidentiality is clear

Calm space, a different space, and a space for reflection, insight, understanding, and resolution

Restorative Solutions always involve a welcome for all parties present and an appreciation that they are there. Hospitality will always be present, food and drink being provided where possible. There is an acknowledgement of the community of care around a wrong-doer by the involvement of friends and family and those who have been affected by his or her doings. The effects of the problem on the lives of all those involved will be named and there is a deliberate focus on making things right for those affected badly by the problem. There is always an affirmation of the student as distinct from the problem;

Restoration may also involve:

An awareness that we have tried a number of interventions before and now we are trying something different

A commitment on the part of school management and staff to encourage the spirit of restitution throughout the entire culture of the school

A recognition by the staff and management of the important linkages between school and community, and an openness to the contributions of persons not usually considered part of the immediate school community

One succinct overview in a criminal justice context states:

Restorative Justice is a process by whereby all the parties with a stake in a particular offence come together to resolve collectively how to deal with the aftermath of the offence and its implications for the future. (Graef 2000)

Restorative Justice aims to restore the balance of a situation disturbed by a crime or conflict and make good the harm caused to the individuals concerned. RJ is a fair process; any outcome must be seen to be just by both parties. RJ is positive and places great emphasis on future. RJ stresses the importance of relationships over rules. RJ seeks at all times to restore the relationships damaged by inappropriate or offensive behaviours.

Understanding the terms

Conferencing

Traditionally conferencing in the UK has been associated with family group conferencing (Zehr, 2003) which involve the young person, family members, supporters of the victim and his / her family and supporters and possibly other community members.

In a school context we refer to small/short conferences (involving pupils only) and full conferences (involving pupils, parents/carers). Full conferences may include any relevant parties and supporters even including community members. These are for more serious occurrences and may relate to things that have extended to problems outside school. For many schools, the need for larger types of conferences would be much less likely.

The common thread in both small and large conferences is the fact that each follows broadly the same structure and format. There is a formality about them with a focus on resolution; the agreements coming from the children themselves. Follow-up is also an important part of the process.

Conferencing is thus a way of bringing two or more people together to address wrongdoing and conflict. All participants are encouraged to speak and express their feelings. All participants have a say in the outcome.

Key elements of a restorative conference:

→ It is voluntary- everyone is there by choice (informed)

→ It brings together the participants

→ The starting position of the facilitator is one of appreciation of the choice that everyone has made to be there

→ It creates a safe and supportive environment

→ It keeps the process focused and records the decisions of the group/pupils

→ The conference facilitator does not make or influence the decisions

→ All participants are encouraged to express themselves and to find their own creative solutions

→ The participants involved are there because they are those directly affected by what has happened

Role of conference facilitators:
Their role is to chair, guide and facilitate the process. They do not control but encourage. They manage, listen, work with silences and effectively chair conferences ensuring everyone's safety and participation.

The conference 'format' otherwise known as "script"
The script is merely a tool, which aids the facilitator in running a conference. It is important for facilitators of restorative conferences to be trained whether or not they use the script. Use of a written format or script may provide a useful tool to those newly trained. Pupils working as Peer facilitators may find the script useful to maintain the focus of the conferences. (Restorative Justice at Ryton Park, DVD, Inclusive Solutions 2003) Some may find it helpful to have key points and notes in a handbook form or on cards. (See Chapters 6 and 7 for detail)

Conferences can be scripted or unscripted:
This depends upon the favoured model and the experience of the trainer. We have all relied on set formats or prompt sheets or 'scripts' when starting out with this way of working.

In both scripted and unscripted the series of questions asked should follow a meaningful progression. All questions are open ended to encourage participants to:

→ Describe what happened.

→ Express how they felt.

→ Say how they were affected by the issue that bought them together.

→ Exchange ideas.

→ Arrive at an agreement.

→ Plan to address the conflict or wrongdoing.

→ Repair the harm.

Mediation

A mediator can be involved where the two parties do not want to meet face to face, restorative conversations can occur with each of the parties thoughts/feelings and wishes being relayed via a third party. Mediation also describes a process where no one party is clearly in the wrong and an impartial facilitator listens to both sides of the story and the feelings of both parties. The parties are ultimately asked what they can do to resolve the situation. Peer mediators are particularly powerful in this intervention. (Peer Mediators at Gladehill, DVD, Inclusive Solutions 2003)

Restorative circles

Restorative circles involve working with a group of pupils where an issue has been identified. This can take the form of whole class groups where appropriate. Preparing the group by exercises and scenarios to help their thinking and understanding is important here.

Restorative Enquiry

Restorative enquiry uses restorative questions and empathic listening to explore a situation. It may be needed for example as part of a mini interview around a conference.

Restorative Dialogue/Discussion

Restorative discussion or dialogue uses restorative questions and reflections. Two or more people are led through a process to elicit more information and sometimes to find out whether the pupil/parent/carer is willing to meet the other party.

Restorative Conversation

A simple exchange making use of restorative language reflecting on feelings, impact of actions and the future.

Restorative Short Conference

A facilitator works with those most immediately involved in the conflict. This may only involve three people, the facilitator, victim and offender. Small conferences may also be needed in the lead up to a large conference or as a way to hold a large group meeting.

Restorative Full Conference

This will involve as many of the stakeholders and supporters involved in the incident as feasible, including the pupils involved and significant others such as parents, carers, teachers and other stakeholders impacted upon. The conference is a coming together to talk about what happened, who has been affected and what can be done to put things right.

The four R's :

Responsibility - by being involved in the restorative process children and young people are learning what it means to be responsible for their own behaviour.

Reintegration - is emphasised, rather than exclusion through punishment.

Reparation - a key feature of reparation is the involvement and consultation of all participants, especially the person who has been harmed particularly if there is a clear "victim".

Rights - is the fourth "r", the right to be safe and feel safe in a community/school and the right to "have a say" and actively participate in decisions.

"Victims" and "offenders"

Why we need to take care with our language

As we look at the background and wider context of RJ we will consider how the principles, approaches and methods have transferred to schools. Our language needs to be carefully considered when used in a school setting. For example, "victim"/"offender" which is central to the language of criminal justice, do not really fit an environment where children and young people are learning how to be together.

Both terms are potentially stigmatising and we prefer to focus on what has been done, in what context, by whom, to whom, who has been affected, what needs to happen to put things right and how that will look in action.

This way of talking provides much more scope for children and young people to be able to learn and move on from undesirable behaviours and not get stuck in positions or with unhelpful labels.

Wrongdoing

Restorative thinking is based upon older understandings of wrongdoing, common to many ancient and traditional societies. Put simply, our ancestors would understand wrongdoing as put by Howard Zehr (2002):

Crime is a violation of people and interpersonal relationships

Violations create obligations

The central obligation is to put right the wrongs

What Restorative Solutions are not:

→ Not about administering of rewards and punishments

→ Not about physical restraint, exclusion or criticism

→ Not just about mediation or listening although there are elements of both within the restorative process

→ Not Social Skills training, although new skills of communication may be learned

→ Not about directly teaching a set of skills such as conflict management or emotional literacy, although these skills are inherent in the restorative process

→ Not 'therapy', although they may have a therapeutic effect

→ Not conflict resolution, although the restorative process can resolve conflicts.

So...

If we are serious about listening to young people, being truly child and relationship centred, we will need to increasingly involve and listen to the most marginalised individuals equally.

> Living on the margin either burns you out and kills you or it turns you into a dreamer, someone who really knows what sort of change will help and who can just about taste it; someone who is prepared to do anything to bring about change. If these dreamers are liberated, if they are brought into the arms of society, they become the new architects of the new community; a community that has a new capacity to support everyone's needs and interactions. (Judith Snow, 1993)

Finally, a key concept for RJ is that everyone ends up stronger not weaker as a result of the process. This includes the young person who has caused harm, whatever they have done. They will be stronger and their self esteem will not be reduced because they have truly learned something important, they have learned about the actual and emotional impact of their actions and they have put things right.

Teaching our pupils to mediate, to restore relationships rather than resorting to power tactics or force can only be a source of hope for the future. What have we learned from our past ways of dealing with difficult behaviour? Traditional methods seem to involve a range of strategies with only limited impact and too often caught within the "straight jacket" of rewards and punishments. We need world-changing tools if we really want the world to change and become safer and more peaceful. Where better to start than in our schools?

'Cowardice asks the question: is it safe? Expediency asks the question: is it politic? Vanity asks the question: is it popular? But conscience asks the question: is it right? And there comes a time when one must take a position that is neither safe, nor politic, nor popular - but one must take it because it's right'

Martin Luther King

Building a Restorative Ethos

This chapter looks at:

→ Promoting a restorative approach to schools, teachers and members of staff, pupils and their parents and carers

→ The research base

→ Questioning existing responses to behaviour

→ Understanding Change – The Medicine Wheel

→ Phase 1 - Leadership

→ Phase 2 - Creating the Vision

→ Phase 3 - Engaging the Community

→ Phase 4 - Implementation and management

Promoting a Restorative Approach in Schools

Belinda Hopkins (2004) in her work promotes a "whole school approach" for a school that is serious about working restoratively. She suggests that restorative interventions need to be fully integrated processes that impact upon day-to-day incidents occurring in any school.

This is a very useful concept to hold as an ideal. However, adopting a "whole school approach" may feel like a huge and unrealistic leap for many schools. Your own school's "ethos" or "culture" is something that has developed and become ingrained over time. It will have a historical context and will echo with stories, predominant views and ideas about education. There will be longstanding heroes and villains. Many views will be held on behaviour, sanctions, punishment and the whole plethora of activity that surrounds school life and relationships.

None of these can change overnight and we are not proposing a Restorative Approach as an either/or option, but as one that can initially run alongside existing discipline policies and procedures. This can evolve towards a more integrated and developmental change addressing at its core some of the more entrenched and fundamental problems of exclusion. Restorative interventions give schools options in their responses to the various behaviours that constitute rule breaking in schools. There needs to be a "fit" between the introduction of restorative solutions and the prevailing culture at some level. This in itself may be a major challenge, when we consider how many stakeholders are involved if a serious incident occurs in a school. These may include: the board of governors, staff, parents, other pupils, and even the media and the audience in the 'outside world.' At times the overwhelming "popular" demand and certainly society's expectations are situated in a retributive mindset, one of punishment and blame. The challenge to any school in developing restorative processes, is therefore, how do we step outside of the punishment/blame frame to make a space for a more collaborative way of restoring relationships?

Considering the research base

One of the first questions any decision maker will have to address when introducing restorative interventions will be; "Does this actually work and where is the evidence in terms of changing attitudes, beliefs and ultimately behaviour towards others?" For schools in the UK, who have pioneered working restoratively, there has not been the luxury of a substantial research base specific to schools. This is now changing and a growing body of national and international research is available to those who need it.

We will provide a summary of some of this research in Chapter 8. For now let us say that the research is optimistic about the effectiveness of Restorative Approaches. For example, here is the summary quotation from an evaluation of a pilot project funded by Scottish Government involving 18 primary, secondary and special schools over a 30-month period in 2005. They found evidence of real transformations in thinking and practice in some schools and significant change across all the schools.

Our evaluation indicates that it (Restorative Approaches) has a great deal to offer. Restorative approaches can be seen to work at all levels of the school, with all students including those in trouble or conflict. It can be seen to support staff as well as students and is non-pathologizing – students do not need to be labelled. It promotes student and staff participation in school processes, promoting the student voice... the new overall concept, the structuring of the skills and strategies into a coherent framework underpinned by a strong value base clearly offers something distinctive that schools can be enthusiastic about and can use as a basis to renew and develop their culture.' (Lloyd, 2005)

Research with other groups, has confirmed far-reaching implications for learning about the consequences of behaviour on others (Maxwell and Morris, 1993, Jackson, 1998). The opportunities presented by a restorative process for young people to take responsibility for repairing harm caused by their actions have been seen to be equally effective in educational settings. Such opportunities are likely to be also transferable to any family or residential community. Some of the unique outcomes are: the reduction of fear, enhancement of harmonious relationships, potential for learning and an enhancement of self esteem acquired by the real sense of achievement and resolution for all those concerned (Hopkins, 2004, Drewery, 2002).

Questioning existing responses to behaviour

Promoting restorative practice in school communities and elsewhere will require some serious challenge to what happens currently within discipline systems. Staff teams will need to think together about the shortcomings of current practice when they deal with challenging behaviour and relationships.

How do we respond to behaviour? How effective is this response? How can we improve our practice in maximising children's learning when it comes to behaviour in relation to others? These are just some of the key questions on the starting "rung" for a school intent on moving up the restorative ladder.

Consider your own position

Imagine you have been hurt emotionally or physically....
Someone has really annoyed you by his or her actions.
Someone has stolen from you, or vandalised a precious possession of yours.
Something has made you really angry.

So now let us consider:

How do you want to be treated when you get very angry?

We would guess that you would definitely not want the following:

> **To be physically restrained**
> **To be shouted at**
> **To be punished**
> **To be locked up somewhere**
> **To be placed in a small bare room**
> **To be excluded**
> **To be sent away from where you live or work to be with other people who also lose their temper**
> **To be segregated in a small special unit**

Based on what many people have told us in response to these questions, we would guess you would prefer one or more of the following things to happen:

> **To be left alone for a while**
> **To be given space**
> **To be allowed to shout very loudly at someone - to vent your feelings to a good listener**
> **To be able to tell someone what happened to make you feel angry**
> **To talk about how you might be feeling now**
> **To have a quiet time with someone you really trust**
> **To fully express your feelings**
> **To be able to "let off steam" safely - until you feel calmer**
> **To be allowed to give your account without being judged**
> **To be listened to**
> **To be provided with an opening in order to move on**

What do you think? Do you feel that this works better for you than the first list? Do you notice anything? Perhaps you notice that the first list represents what we do to lots of children and young people all over the UK virtually every day when their emotions overwhelm them.

Do you think we could provide our young people who find themselves very angry more of the second list?

Could we allow more opportunities for our young people to respond in a different way? Would we be beginning to move in a more restorative, responsive and respectful direction if we did?

Understanding Change – The Medicine Wheel

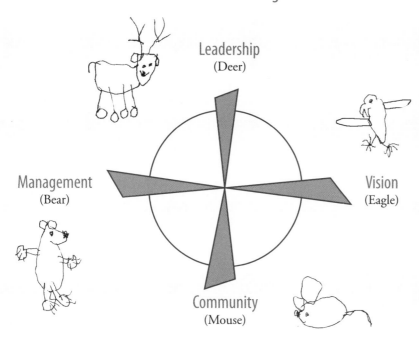

The Deer looks down from the mountain and leads the herd

The Eagle soars high and sees the whole picture below and ahead

Mice scurry around busily together building community

Bears lumber slowly but makes things happen

Harrison Owen in his work on 'Open Space Technology' depicts the ancient Medicine Wheel as above (Owen, 2003). This is derived from centuries of tradition among First Nation Americans and has informed many cultures in different ways. We find this an extremely powerful metaphor for understanding the process of organisational change and renewal.

The wheel of change begins in the north with a leading idea, for us - Restorative Solutions. Travelling clockwise to the east we develop a shared vision of what this could look like in schools and communities. Then moving south we ask who needs to come with us on the journey. We wish to take as many community members along with us as we can. In a school, this would mean enrolling the support of head, governors, senior managers, the wider staff group, parents and ultimately pupils. Finally, at the west, we manage and implement the idea. We take action and turn the Restorative Solutions into reality.

The cycle of this medicine wheel is an excellent way to view change processes for any team, organisation or community. When we contemplate change, the risk is always that we will jump prematurely from the big ideas (leadership) to practice (management) and ignore the other two important phases of creating vision and engaging the wider community.

Phase One - Leadership

I've heard of this great idea, and it's being used around the country in some leading schools, let's change our school culture to one which is restorative, making relationships a priority and putting rewards and sanctions into the background. (Infant School Head Teacher, Nottingham City)

A successful leader may set the conditions in which the seeds of a great idea will grow. The leader knows exactly how to plant the seed, tend, feed and water it to best effect whatever soil and weather they are working with.
It begins with an idea. The seed is planted with enough authority or support to ensure it will grow.

The seeds are in place.... (Anon)

Someone must lead or nothing will happen. Perhaps we do not always need the support from the most senior levels of a school or organisation, but it will be harder if we do not have this. Myron Rogers, viewing organisations as living networks and change processes as energy, is quoted by Wheatley (2005) as saying simply 'Start change anywhere and follow it everywhere'.

In all schools there was evidence of strong enthusiasm and commitment on the part of key staff and, in some, of real transformation of thinking and practice. Visible commitment on the part of school managers and key enthusiasts was highly significant in promoting changing practice—other interviewees identified modeling by senior and key staff as central to their own development. (Lloyd, 2005)

Questions 'Leaders' will need to ask themselves

Questions both on an organisational level and individual level that need to be considered include the following:

What sort of space are you trying to create, both as a school and as someone who practices restorative approaches? This relates to the operational aspects, the physical environment and also to the space in yourself that might allow you to think and, more importantly, to act from a restorative practitioner position.

How are you going to "model" being a restorative practitioner "walking the talk"? For instance, how and when will you be facilitating conferences, promoting restorative interventions, running restorative circles? It is also important to consider how this will "fit" with the expectations of your existing role.

As a Head Teacher or senior manager, can you step into the neutral space required to facilitate a restorative conference and would the participants be able to accept such a difference in your role? If not, what explanation and preparation might they need?

Who should introduce these new ways of thinking and working? In some schools, staff members at less senior levels have seen it implemented in other school settings and presented the ideas and concept of working restoratively as a proposal in their own settings. In other areas, Local Education Departments have taken the lead and training has been cascaded to schools within a borough, region or county. Other schools have been involved in projects piloted as initiatives by the Youth Justice Board and later extended across England, Northern Ireland, Wales and Scotland. Perhaps Youth Offending Teams or visiting Support Services have introduced the Restorative Approach into schools.

From our experience and the available research it seems essential in all schools for Restorative Approaches to be heralded by Head Teachers. They need to be instrumental in setting up training and in creating a starting point for strategic planning and follow-up. Cascade training has also been effective - a range of staff members, some Senior Management Team, Pastoral and some Behaviour support, have been trained to implement the model and, once familiar with it, train other members of staff.

In some cases, a restorative coordinator has been assigned to lead on a range of tasks. As part of an organisational strategy it is useful to have in place a core-working group of committed and enthusiastic members of staff. The group can share the tasks and support each other, promote restorative practices and share and extend ideas about what might work in a particular setting.

So someone has named the idea - where next?

Gandhi was reversing the materialistic concept that conditions determine psychology. No, psychology could shape conditions. 'What you think, you become.' (The life of Mahatma Gandhi, Louis Fischer, 1982)

Phase Two – Creating Shared Vision

The second phase is about considering the ethos/culture that defines your school at present.

How would we like to see this change?

Who else is a stakeholder in this different future?

Are you aiming for a shared vision that all can buy into?

What value base is it rooted in?

What blue-sky thoughts are associated with the future?

This vision or dream space is not grounded in reality but reaches for a changed world. So take care in this stage of the Medicine Wheel and resist the temptation to create flow diagrams or write outcomes. If you need these they can be done later when we are in the 'Management' phase of the wheel.

Martin Luther King reached for a dream, a dream of racial equality in the States, a dream he perhaps never thought he would see realised in his own lifetime. It was genuinely a dream and most definitely not a set of aims and objectives.

A shared vision can be developed through dialogue, by effective communication or developing a shared graphic or visual dream through a facilitated process such as used in Person Centred Planning and systemic thinking.

What are the steps we could take to make the difference to the quality of relationships/ behaviour and, ultimately, all those involved in the community of the school? A core team need to visualise how this might look in their school and have a clear idea of how it might be implemented and developed. The commitment to it starts here.

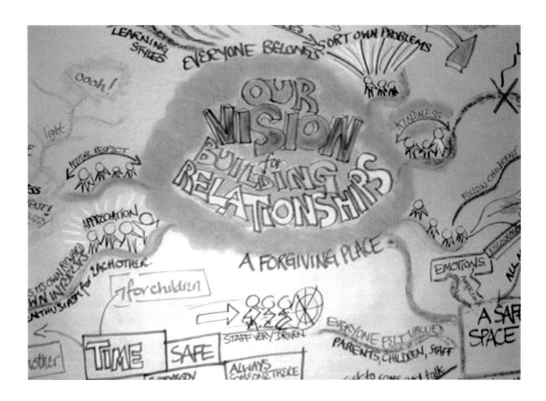

How can all those involved in the school community; from head teacher through to midday meals supervisor, board of governors through to pupils and their families have a stake in the workings of the school?

Listening, empathy, being non-judgemental, personal and civic responsibilities are all integral to restorative approaches and PSHE and citizenship. This therefore could ensure a firm grounding in the school that will allow for a restorative vision and change of culture. It should be enabling and inclusive to pupils.

The vision needs to be articulated through maximum participation and recorded, ideally visually, on a large graphic that can be displayed and returned to regularly.

So you have developed a shared vision of what a restorative school ethos could mean.

Phase Three – Taking the community with you

People only support what they create. Life insists on its freedom to participate and can never be coerced into accepting someone else's plans. (Wheatley, 2005)

Who will you need to take with you? This is a crucial stage. Who are the key stakeholders in the change towards a more restorative school? How can you best enrol their support?

Wheatley (2005) argues that we should abandon mechanistic assumptions about organisational change as meaning behaves more like energy. So we do not have to achieve a critical mass, or roll out programmes across a whole school. Instead we can work locally finding creative ideas that are meaningful to one area of the system. Energy generated here will lead to other networks taking notice.

She argues strongly for engaging participation processes when undergoing change. We should involve everybody who cares and anyone likely to be affected by changes.

We haven't yet absorbed the simple truth that we can't force anybody to change. We can only involve them in the change process from the beginning and see what's possible. If change becomes meaningful to them, they will change. If we want their support, we must welcome them as co-creators.

(Wheatley, 2005)

Perhaps a starting point here is to ask some fundamental questions that will test your school's commitment to the "vision". Is there is a willingness for the school to consider these questions:

Has harm been done? How often and to whom?

Is there a need to repair the harm? By who?

Do we have the time to make this an investment in our school?

Can we afford not to?

Is the meaning of this work clear?

Who is missing?

Who else needs to do this work?

Are we sharing information more openly?

Are we becoming more honest with each other?

Building on the desire to introduce restorative practices into your setting, this vision to move this forward should be based upon a clear understanding of the principles of restorative justice and what it would mean "in action".

The vision will provide the foundation upon which to build and develop restorative principles into the school's policy and practice.

Who needs to be involved?

In cases where schools are working with external agencies to set up and input into restorative interventions, clear arrangements concerning how this will be delivered will need to be made. Negotiating clear agreements, expectations and protocols between the school and agencies involved will be an essential part of this process.

Questions for this phase may include:

> Who will be responsible for what?

> Where is the expertise necessary to develop restorative practices?

> How will these interventions be delivered in this setting?

Raising Staff Awareness

Less than half of the programme schools (11 out of 26) had integrated restorative approaches into the school behaviour policy. Most of the schools that had integrated restorative approaches were still in the process of revising their behaviour policies, so it was not possible to ascertain the degree to which restorative justice had been integrated.

Thorough integration of any approach to behaviour improvement is essential if it is to be an effective whole-school approach. The positive results from the pupil survey of the Blackpool non-programme school suggests that any thoroughly implemented positive whole-school behaviour policy can be effective. Restorative justice is unlikely to be fully effective unless thoroughly implemented whole-school behaviour policies are in place and transmitted to staff through INSET. (Youth Justice Board, 2004)

We would suggest participative conversations with staff teams at all levels from senior management forums to staff INSET days. It may also be politic to offer a presentation of restorative principles and how they might work in your school to the board of governors and parents forums. In these cases, think about the issues that are specific to your school and some of the patterns of behaviour that could be impacted upon by a restorative approach. Bring this alive with some pertinent case examples and restorative strategies that have already been effective elsewhere. Stories are a very powerful way of triggering insights and change.

Involving Parents and Pupils

Be proactive. Talk to pupils and parents at every opportunity about this new way of working. Make use of handouts/leaflets and newsletters. When they know about this way of working pupils or parents may wish to request a restorative intervention or participate at the request of another party.

Successful schools:

→ Write to parents.

→ Produce leaflets on Restorative Solutions.

→ Set up meetings to launch and explain the new approach.

→ Use opportunities such as parents' evenings, open days and other school events to answer questions and give information to parents and carers.

→ Explain in detail what is happening to those involved in conferencing.

→ Spend time in preparation.

Engaging the wider local Community

UK communities have changed. Historically, in post war Britain mutual support and connection were well-recognised aspects of traditional community organisation with a strong spirit of looking out for other locality members and neighbours. Unlocked doors were a symbol in many areas of trust and openness. As we have moved into the 21st century the community life many children grow up in is very different. Many families are much more insular, inward looking, with safety and distrust being often uppermost in the concerns of community members. Concerns for potential abusers, violence and criminality may prevent carers from allowing children to play outside independently let alone leave doors unlocked. At the same time many communities have also become increasingly diverse places culturally and in other respects and as a result much more interesting and exciting. Communities may be full of problems and tensions but they are also brimming with possibility.

In response to many of the problems faced in our communities well-intentioned leaders are taking one of two very divergent paths.

The first which begins by focusing on a communities needs, deficiencies and problems is still by far the most travelled and commands the vast majority of our financial and human resources. By comparison, is the second path, which insists on beginning with a clear commitment to discovering a community's capacities and assets. (Kretzman and Knight, 1993)

Reading about or watching media coverage of deprived inner city communities and rural pockets of disadvantage provide overwhelmingly negative images. Unemployment, drugs, violent crime, homelessness and so on all provide us with images of problematic and deficient communities full of deficient and needy people.

A more productive and positive approach for leaders is to focus less on the needs of a community and more on the capacities, skills and assets of community members including lower income people and the localities in which they live.

Focus on the Gifts of the Community

Leaders serious about community engagement will map out the assets of a community including local institutions, associations to which local people belong and the actual gifts of individuals.

Places may include:

→ Hospitals
→ Colleges
→ Libraries
→ Parks
→ Churches/places of worship
→ Other schools
→ Early years settings
→ Work Places

Associations may include:

→ Community development organisations
→ Church groups
→ Community groups
→ Early Years groups
→ Out of school clubs
→ Mentoring organisations
→ Youth clubs
→ Drama/Arts groups
→ Uniformed organisations (e.g. Scouts/Boys Brigade)

Individual gifts of community members may include:

→ Leadership skills and experiences
  (e.g. running a playgroup/drama group/local society)
→ Specific skills e.g. artistic/crafts/fishing/gardening
→ Hospitality
→ Friendship
→ Inspiration
→ Years of experience
→ Generosity with time and/or resources

Bringing up challenging children is more than any one person's work, more than one parent, more than one teacher. Leaders need to harness the capacities that exist beyond the school building to enhance life opportunities, provide role models and a richer range of life experiences than a school could ever provide. Simply involving the elders in a community in the lives of the most troubled individuals can be a very powerful way of changing behaviour and meeting unmet emotional needs.

Enlisting Community Involvement

Historically it is clear that significant community development only takes place when local people are committed to investing themselves and their people in the effort. Top down community building or even outside in tends not to work. School leaders are uniquely placed inside communities and have powerful opportunities to lead and facilitate change. Local people will unite very powerfully around shared concerns or agreed aims and this can be a very powerful force given effective leadership. Behaviour and relationships can provide that shared focus.

Every head will be aware of how the wider community can get involved in matters of 'wrong doing'. The community may condone, condemn or create the conditions which maximise opportunities in which rule breaking is either more or less likely. The challenge for school leaders trying to work more restoratively is to harness some of the power of their local community and to positively engage them in the change process. It is interesting to note the linkage between the theme of community engagement in change and the 'Headteacher Standards' and Standard 6 - Strengthening Community in particular:

Schools exist in a distinctive social context, which has a direct impact on what happens inside the school. School leadership should commit to engaging with the internal and external school community to secure equity and entitlement. Head teachers should collaborate with other schools in order to share expertise and bring positive benefit to their own and other schools. They should work collaboratively at both strategic and operational levels with parents and carers and across multiple agencies for the well-being of all children. Head teachers share responsibility for leadership of the wider educational system and should be aware that school improvement and community development are interdependent."
Head Teacher Standard 6 - Strengthening Community (2006)

Involving parents and the wider community requires proactive work from school leaders plus creativity and excellent communication processes. Working towards "the ideal" the concept of "whole school" extends also to the community. Taking the community with you as you attempt to create a more restorative ethos is not optional. If you are serious, it is essential. Participation is all.

Phase Four - Implementation and Action

If enough quality groundwork has been done in the first three steps of the medicine wheel, then the management stage should almost be starting to shape itself.

With the foundations of leadership, vision and community in place, the model is ready to be put into practice and it will then grow and develop its own momentum. (See also Appendix 3: flow chart, information at requesting involvement stage, agreements/ contract, information sheets to pupils, parents/carers, school staff.)

So who is going to do what and when?

What does the action plan look like?

What resources will be needed?

Where will this work take place and when?

Where will this work be named in the School Development or Improvement Plan?

Systems

Systems need to be in place for implementation and a clear indication of where restorative interventions will be located within the behaviour management process is important. Restorative philosophy and approaches promote working across systems and the weaving together of all aspects of a child's life into an integrated whole. This means everybody is working together towards the same aim. It is no good having a wonderful conference with a resolution and mending of the harm only for that child to walk out and be punished by a member of staff who has not fully understood that amends had been made.

"After 18 months, indicators of success are beginning to emerge. These include:
Clear lead from a schools' Senior Management Team;
An on-going part of a school's development plan over a number of years;
High priority being given to information dissemination and training;
Broad base of practitioners within schools that can support each other and on-going developments;
Range of training opportunities to be made available"
(Peta Barber, Co-ordinator, Restorative Practices, Highland Region, Scotland, 2005)

Systems also need to be in place for:

→ Requesting involvement, record keeping, follow-up and evaluation.

→ Communication systems for the people who are involved in a restorative conference, when and where it is going to happen, whether permission slips are needed (e.g. if a restorative conference takes any time out of a lesson). A restorative bulletin board is one useful way to communicate and keep colleagues up to date about the implementation and development of restorative approaches.

→ Information to all staff members about what restorative practice is all about. An explanation of the different interventions and what to expect from these processes. Information written in the form of leaflets/handouts/posters adapting the language for staff, parents and children should be circulated to all those in the school community who need it. Information can be given in all sorts of creative ways. Students may inform their peers of RJ methods via role-plays at school assemblies and RJ stalls can be made available at parent's evenings and school open days and so forth.

→ Clarity about where information will be stored, what gets shared and confidentiality.

→ Clear and simple stages for all to follow. From the request for a restorative intervention through to follow up will need clarity at every stage to avoid confusion and miscommunication.

Training

Training is also a key part of Phase 4 and should include staff INSET and other training. Whilst a one-day INSET event might set the stage, raise awareness and begin to influence the whole staff culture, opportunities for training those staff members likely to have greatest involvement should be made available. They will need at least 1-5 day's intensive training around the core skills and processes of restorative work, depending on their existing competencies. This may include work on welcoming, preparing, facilitating meetings, empathetic listening, short and full restorative conferencing and other restorative processes.

No-one on the staff really knows about this. Had I not been told by the deputy head, I wouldn't have known about it. (Head of Year)

All we got was a one-minute input at the end of a meeting. (Youth Offending Team staff member)

Making time for INSET on restorative approaches has been the single biggest barrier to implementation. Only 8 of the 26 schools undertook any INSET, and 5 of these were primary schools (four Oxfordshire schools were provided with free one-day consultancy to run INSET and work with staff). (Youth Justice Board, 2004)

Facilitators

A number of well-trained facilitators need to be available to run conferences. Ideally about 10% of staff in a school need to be able to facilitate short or full conferences. One or two short briefings or training workshops are required to equip staff to put forward children for conferences. The more effective this way of working is, the greater the demand for training. To ensure good practice we would advise top - up training and building in regular supervision and support for facilitators.

We have found that for more complex situations two members of staff working to co-facilitate conferences is a useful model in terms of mutual support, time and effective practice.

Support / Supervision / Consultation

School staff will benefit from systematic and regular support and supervision structures. In Hammersmith and Fulham, using an experienced but neutral person to help in more complex conflicts, including large group and teacher/pupil conflicts proved invaluable. Access to and direct involvement of a police officer trained in RJ methods should also be considered for the most serious cases.

At the end of more complex and emotionally demanding conferences, providing a space for the facilitators to debrief and reflect is extremely helpful.

Time

There is also a need to overcome the perception that the process is too time consuming. Although this is undoubtedly true in the short term, the net gains make the process worthwhile and valuable in the longer term. (Alastair McKinlay, Tain Royal Academy, 2006)

Preparation, assessment, the process of running conferences and follow-up are all time consuming activities and a typical budget is as follows:

Approximate Time Frames

→ Short Conference: 20-45 minutes

→ Full Conference: 1-2 hours (preparation involves 20-40 minutes with all key players - 3 hours in total typically)

So staff responsible for delivering the model need adequate time to be set aside. As an alternative, some schools have relied upon outside agencies such as local youth offending teams, police, or other mediation services to deliver restorative conferencing. But even if you do involve external agency support, time will be needed for staff to liaise and do the necessary liaison and follow up work.

Restorative conferences need to be as timely as possible (within a few days of the incident), once all parties are ready to sit and talk in a calm manner. More organising time will be needed should supporters and parents/carers be involved. Recognition of the amount of time the conferences take should be structured into staff members' timetables. There can be no shortcuts in terms of the preparation that is required or the time intensiveness of some of the more complex conferences.

There is no absolute template on time. For example a "gang" dispute spilling into two separate secondary schools involved a thorough process whereby pupils, parents, staff were all consulted. The eventual large group conference that took place at the end of the process was successful because of the time taken to lay the foundations. This is in contrast to the short conference that took place in the playground run by a Teaching Assistant with two pupils locked in a conflict over a football match.

If a full conference is required or there is a need to involve a number of different participants, the process of a restorative conference becomes quite costly in terms of time. The preparation itself may involve interviewing each individual, with the possibility of running some smaller restorative circles. The eventual full restorative conference may take up to two hours and may include refreshment time.

Monitoring / Evaluation / Review

Once a school begins to operate more restoratively you will want to monitor and evaluate what you are doing as fully as possible.
The focus of the monitoring and evaluation are likely to be around:
1. The restorative strategy and its implementation
2. The mechanisms to ensure that agreements made in conferences are adhered to.

This means that the written conference agreements are used to monitor the actual compliance – are people doing what they said they would during the conference? Some practitioners favour interviewing conference participants 2 and 6 weeks after any conference.

Essential questions to be considered at each point of the setting up and delivery process are:

→ What outcomes are we seeking to achieve?

→ What is the quality of our decision-making?

→ Are we using every opportunity to educate young people about the consequences of their actions on others as well as themselves?

→ Are we providing children and young people with helpful alternatives to their existing harmful behaviours?

→ Who needs to know what has been achieved in a conference and who can reinforce/endorse the positive behaviours in school/at home/in the community?

Signs that a school is beginning to think restoratively

If a member of the senior management team is acting restoratively the questions asked in the wake of any incident would be:

What has happened?

Who is responsible/accountable?

Who has been affected?

What might their needs be?

What is the extent of harm done?

How might we begin to repair the harm?

Running parallel to this would be:

Who can help this process?

How can we help the young person face up to the wrong/harm done?

Who are the best people to do that and are we giving them the adequate time to do it properly?

One of our head Teachers describes how much 'calmer' her school has become since Restorative Approaches were embedded within her School Development Plan and ethos builders. The number of incidents logged has declined and, yes, things do go awry but there is a confidence that the outcomes are likely to be positive.

Maybe that is it - with Restorative Approaches schools can become calmer and pleasanter places to be. A key task will be to roll out to the wider school community the lessons learned from the pilot. (Mike Ciesla, Fife Council Education Service, December 2006)

'In taking revenge, a man is but
even with his enemy; but in
passing it over he is superior'

Francis Bacon

In this chapter we cover:

→ Preparing for restorative working

→ Assessing which intervention to use

→ Suitability and Seriousness

→ Preparation for a restorative conference

→ A restorative vignette

→ Decisions to be made

→ Traffic Light System for triggering Conferences

→ Final reminder on basic restorative position

Preparation for Working Restoratively

Whilst the word assessment may sound rather formal, a restorative assessment is a two way process whereby the young person and participants assess whether they can "buy into" the process. It is about empowering the young person to make an informed choice.

We recommend a Preparation/Assessment framework that addresses four key areas: Suitability, Safety, Seriousness and Participation

Suitability / Fit

The assessment is a process of matching your restorative intervention to the rule breaking incident. It is essential to take into account pupil choice and consent when considering a restorative conference. If a teacher requests a conference for two pupils who have been in conflict, but one does not wish to be involved this would have to be passed back to the teacher who made the request to make a decision about it. This might leave the issue still live and the adults facing their own choices of future action.

There also has to be a fit for a child or young person. If they feel that sides will be taken it is unlikely that the conference will work. It is important that the member of staff who facilitates the restorative conference is perceived by the child as neutral and objective. This can be challenging if the teacher's job also includes sanctioning, but this issue is not insurmountable if boundaries are clearly set out by those involved.

Safety

One of the highest priorities in schools is to maintain safety in and around the school. An integral aspect of this is ensuring that each member of the school community can act in a civil manner towards each other. If a child has experienced different forms of ongoing intimidation from a group of children, it is unlikely to be safe to expose that child to a group conference. However a restorative conference could be effective in addressing the issues with the children in question without directly exposing the child who has been on the receiving end of this in the meeting. Alternatively it may be that the child would actually wish to be involved in a restorative conference. In this case each child involved could need to be seen separately and assessments made. A series of one to one conferences might then follow on from this if appropriate and judged as safe.

A full conference would likely involve the person harmed and their parent or carers and the main instigator and their parent or carers first and then an assessment of what other conferences need to take place and with whom. It is important to ensure the 'power balance' is as equal as possible and that no one feels more powerful because they have more supporters present.

To reiterate, in cases where one child has been on the receiving end of taunts and put downs by two or more pupils, it is very important to keep the short conferences one-to-one and even. This might require the victim to be involved in more than one conference on a one to one basis; however equity is maintained. Our feedback demonstrates that a child who has been victimised has felt on more of an equal footing in a one to one conference and it has been an empowering experience.

The preparation and assessment phase importantly should pick up issues of child protection. If however there is no such indication and a comment or disclosure is made in a conference that a child or someone else is at harm or at risk of harm, it would not be appropriate to pursue this in the conference itself. Further exploration of this would need to be followed up immediately after the conference. Child Protection procedures would need to be followed in the usual way in line with national and local expectations.

This highlights the importance of being clear at the beginning of a conference about confidentiality and the provisos. An integral part of the process is ensuring very early on that basic ground rules are laid. A typical set of ground rules are likely to look like this:

→ Confidentiality unless someone being hurt or in danger

→ Mutual Respect

→ One person speaking at a time

→ No preaching at each other

Seriousness

A caution about "seriousness".

There will be different perspectives on seriousness. Schools will have views, policies and procedures about which behaviours warrant different types and lengths of exclusion. We have found that some great opportunities for individuals to learn and grow into more humane people, can be lost by going down an exclusion route. For some young people this will only serve to add to their already low self-esteem and possibly echo emotional experiences of abandonment, segregation and neglect they may have had as a result.

One way of judging the seriousness of an incident is to refer to your school's existing sanction thresholds. However if this is the only criterion used you will likely not be sensitive to individual pupil's perceptions of how serious the incident was for them. So ultimately it is a judgement call that recognises that seriousness is always relative to the situation of the child in question.

Participation

A significant factor to consider in each case is how far to involve parents and carers and this needs to be discussed very early in the process at the preparation phase. Direct involvement and full participation in a conference is generally to be welcomed. Alternatively indirect involvement would mean they would be kept informed of what was happening, the decisions made and the agreements and actions decided upon within the conference.

When considering who has been affected by an incident, parents/carers and siblings can often be overlooked by school staff whose main focus is the pupils directly involved in an incident. Families can form an important part of the reconciliation process and can help to reinforce a child's positive behaviours in schools.

Preparation for a restorative conference

The importance of the pre-conference work cannot be over stated. Proper preparation will ensure a safe and effective conference. In essence, preparation is about giving each person space to think about what sort of outcome they would like and the part they can play in attaining it. This is framed in a positive way by an invitation or welcome (not a summons) to those involved to be part of the preparation process. You should explain to each person how the conference will work and allow time for questions and or worries to be aired. The goals of the conference should be made explicit in this preparatory work, as is the expectation that each participant will respect each other. This may be tough when there are angry feelings or very different perspectives on the incident present. You will need to:

→ Create a checklist for preparation

→ Explain the purpose of restorative conference

→ Prepare people for what will happen

→ Hear their story – what has happened

→ Model and explain how things will be in the conference

(See Chapters 6 and 7 for detailed sample scripts for these steps)

Case Vignette

Here we outline the **preparation phase** using the case example of
Natalie, a 14 Year old pupil.

*A 14 year old girl Natalie had been friendly with another girl in her year -
Tanya. They "fell out" when a third girl became friendlier with Tanya. Natalie
began to be on the receiving end of nasty comments about her clothes and how
she looked. In many lessons Tanya and the third girl started to comment on how
Natalie smelled and other pupils in the class found this funny.*

*Natalie began to refuse to go to school and her mother had to take time off work
and was at risk of losing her job. Natalie felt the problem escalating in her head
the longer she stayed off. The other girls were oblivious of the distress caused and
effects of what they considered, to be "a bit of a laugh" They had no idea why
Natalie had not returned to school.*

In this case, there was a lot of restorative groundwork and preparation to be done
with Natalie, before she felt ready to come face to face with the other girl. This
involved meeting with her on several occasions over a two-month period, for about
30 minutes each time to listen to her and to give her a clear sense of what would
happen in the conference. She needed reassurances regarding the safety of what
would take place and that she would not be further embarrassed and hurt by the
other two girls.

A crucial part of the assessment involved identifying Tanya's attitude to what
had been happening, which involved guilty, defensive and resentful feelings. It
was important to be sure she was going to be able to be restorative with Natalie.
There was a also need to work at Natalie's pace about when she felt ready for the
conference to take place. If these factors had been neglected it may have been
experienced as a further abuse and violation.

After the conference Natalie's mother commented:

I wasn't sure about my daughter and the bully being in the
same room because I didn't want her upset any more than
she already was. It was months before she was ready but once
she confronted the person she felt much better about it. She
is much stronger now. At first I wanted the child punished
because she hurt my daughter but she was spoken to in a
serious way and she knew I was upset and that she upset
Natalie. The meeting and the contract has worked for my
daughter.

See Appendix 5 for a full commentary on this short conference.

Restorative
Solutions

Decisions to be made

Who needs to attend?

The context in which an incident has occurred and who has been affected will determine who should be present at the conference. In theory, there is no limit to those who could, potentially, be invited in a large conference and this may include; youth workers/YOT staff/counsellors/friends/other school staff. Also, the main two young people most involved can bring a support person of his or her choice. This can be a friend who can help the process.

Consent

Each person involved needs to give their consent to take part. This is a voluntary process. Young people must not feel coerced, no matter how committed you are to the process and the perceived benefits of this way of working. It may be helpful to lay down all of the possible alternatives to a restorative conference and discuss these with the pupil.

Acceptance of Responsibility

There must be a willingness to participate on the part of the person causing the harm. He or she must show some willingness to make amends or some capacity to shift and reflect upon the impact of their actions.

If the young person does not accept responsibility or is looking to blame someone else, this is likely to mean that this conference should not go ahead.

Who will facilitate?

A trained facilitator is required. The facilitator should not have a relationship with either young person, as it may then be perceived that they are not neutral. Advocacy for either side does not fit this model of restoration.

Who should do the restorative assessment and preparation for a conference?

Ideally this would be the facilitator or, if co-facilitating, this task can be shared between the two facilitators. Care must be taken to avoid allegiances with any particular party. If this proves unrealistic then another member of staff, such as pastoral team member may do this first phase of the work. This person must also be trained in working restoratively and will need to follow the preparation process very closely with the person who will be facilitating the conference. Ultimately the facilitator will be the one who coordinates each interaction and the whole process of assessment and person preparation.

Note: Preparation for a conference should never take the place of a conference proper. Care must be taken not to take pupils through the full process at this stage. As a facilitator, you do not need detailed account you just need to know what actually occurred from the different perspectives. You must have a sense that the person wants to resolve things and feel confident you can keep the conference safe for everyone.

Truce Systems

Using a **truce system** as part of a group conference preparation.

A truce system can be a very effective way of managing the period when you are preparing pupils for the conference. Making agreements between pupils to keep to a "truce" can ensure both parties can "save face". Whilst preparations are being made parties can continue to interact around the school in a civil way until things "get sorted". If we think of the example used earlier of the inter-group conflict between two schools, the types of truce agreements that were made included: "not to diss each other in the street", "no dirty looks", "to steer clear of each other". We have even given out truce cards for pupils who are share classes and are useful to children as a reminder to keep the peace.

It is important to have clear time frames and expectations about where and when the conference will be held and how pupils will manage without getting into conflict up to that point. Pupils often like the idea of summits to talk through situations before reaching a crisis point.

Small conference or Full conference?

Facilitators, working closely with key staff, pupils and family members will need to use all their experience and skills to judge when a full conference is needed.

> A Full conference may be required when the young person causing the harm has been doing so over a period of time.

> If it appears that the harm is being carried out intentionally then this would also strengthen the case for a full conference involving parents and other key stakeholders.

> Another significant factor to consider is whether the victim's parent/carer want to be involved. This would be made clear in the preparation and assessment phase. Sometimes parents/carers and siblings can be overlooked by schools who may hold the view that only pupils directly involved in an incident have been affected. The Partners in Evaluation research (2004) found only a small number of large/full conferences taking place in schools at the time of writing and one could speculate about the reasons for this. Our own view is that the involvement of families is crucial for schools that are serious about embracing the reconciliation processes we are exploring in this book.

> If an incident has impacted on a wider web of relationships such as a pupils' friendships across a class or Year group.

> If a permanent exclusion is a likely alternative, then a full conference is likely to be needed to underline the seriousness of the situation.

Is one conference enough?

There will be a very small minority of children whose needs are so great that a single restorative conference alone will not be enough, although it can still be of great value. Each conference can be viewed as a significant learning experience for all involved, particularly those who need to change most. As with all learning we cannot expect one meeting to do everything however great the teaching. At other times the scale of the incident, such as conflicts involving pupils from other schools, will mean that more than one conference is required.

Traffic Light System for triggering Conferences

To Conference or not to Conference? That is the Question

In the preparation and assessment stage the following 'traffic light tool' may help you decide whether or not to go ahead with a conference.

RED -
Conference cannot go ahead when:

→ A pupil has not consented to a conference. This will be either the person who has done the harm or the person on the receiving end. This may be an indication that a pupil needs more time or preparation before committing to this process but clearly this would need to be done within an agreed timescale.

→ There is a refusal to take any responsibility for actions on the part of the person who has caused the harm.

→ There is no acknowledgement of parts played in a conflict and it is unclear where main responsibility for causing harm caused rests.

→ A pupil/parent does not understand what the conference is all about or what it is trying to achieve.

→ A pupil who has done the harm has agreed but is making threats (directly or second hand) to the pupil who has been harmed.

→ The numbers of supporters are uneven (anything other than a small pupil to pupil conference will need to have an equal number of supporters).

→ Someone is judged to be highly likely to be extremely angry, or who will not be able to manage or contain their anger in a way that is safe, at the conference.

AMBER –

Sometimes there is an inbetween stage when more needs to happen before a conference can go ahead. This will often be when:

→ It is not clear whether a conference can go ahead at the preparation stage. There may be indications that it is possible to conference but a pupil may not be quite ready on one or more of the areas named in the Red Light section above.

→ More restorative preparation needs to be done with an individual about learning to take responsibility for their actions.

→ The person who has been harmed does not feel quite ready for a conference.

→ A person needs time to think or talk to parent/carer before committing to the process. In this way you are encouraging them to make an informed choice.

→ Someone may need more assurances and reassurances or simply more information.

→ More time is needed for all parties to buy into the process. Of course, decisions will have to be made if the situation arises where there are uneven numbers for each party. In order to maintain equal numbers, those in the group with most potential supporters can be invited to choose one or more members to step down.

GREEN –

A Conference can go ahead when:

→ All participants have been seen, are fully aware of what a conference is about and what it is trying to achieve.

→ All have agreed to attend by choice.

→ All have had the information they require to make that choice.

→ There is some acknowledgement of responsibility.

→ All are aware of what will be required to ensure safety and respect during the conference.

Using the RED, AMBER, GREEN guide to conference decision-making

The case example used to demonstrate the preparation process on page 64 shows how a school used a restorative approach to reach a pupil whose difficulties with another pupil had become invisible following the other pupil's exclusion. A request was made to the **restorative school coordinator** to ask if anything could be done about Natalie, a 14 year old who was refusing to attend school. Non school attendance was something that had been identified as a "problem" over the last month. The attendance officer had done everything she could, she had met with Natalie and her Mum and her Mum had done everything to get her back to school. Natalie's Mum had become concerned that she herself would get into trouble and even might be taken to court. She was also very concerned that Natalie would get into trouble.

Natalie's Head of Year asked the **restorative school coordinator** if there was anything that could be done restoratively, as things had become a bit stuck. She had met with Natalie and her mother and Natalie's mother talked about trying to get to "get to the bottom of it". Natalie was adamant that 'stomach pains' were keeping her away from school. Natalie's Mum thought this was a way of avoiding talking about some of the problems she was having with another pupil. She was getting worried that the anxiety of having to go back to school and face this pupil was making Natalie ill. Natalie, however, was reluctant to talk to her Year Head.

The restorative practitioner contacted Natalie's mother and explained her role and her proposal to work restoratively. She asked if she could initially meet with Natalie and her mother to find out what they wanted and how she might help. Natalie's mother was keen for this but Natalie initially refused outright to meet or talk. At this stage the assessment was on RED. It looked like a non starter as Natalie was refusing even to meet the restorative practitioner.

Permission was sought to send some information for Natalie and her Mum about the purpose and process of bringing people together restoratively and the different ways things could be resolved. This was solely for their information. Within a day of receiving this, RED had moved to AMBER, as Natalie agreed to speak with the restorative practitioner and arrangements were made to see Natalie the next day.

In the first restorative interview, which was bound by confidentiality (with the usual provisos), it was important that Natalie felt in control of what she wanted to say. It emerged that Natalie's absences, were rooted in her fear of returning to school. She thought she might be met with taunts and threats by Tanya - another girl in her year.

As more of Natalie's story unfolded, she explained that Tanya had instigated a fight with Natalie, which resulted in Tanya being excluded. Tanya returned to school within a week without anything being done to address Natalie and Tanya's relationship or restore things between them. One of Natalie's fears was that Tanya would come back with more anger towards her, as a result of the exclusion and that she might even get some of her friends involved "to rough her up". Natalie had heard on the grapevine that Tanya "was going to get her, big time" - so she stopped attending just prior to Tanya's return.

The longer Natalie remained absent from school, the greater her fear of Tanya became. Natalie was convinced that Tanya's main focus was on "getting back at her" and "doing her harm". She began to become reluctant to go out of the house at certain times for fear of seeing Tanya's friends, some of whom lived in the area.

To add to this, Natalie's mother put her job at risk because of the amount of time she was taking off to look after Natalie.

After exploring the questions and worries Natalie and her Mum had about attending a restorative meeting with Tanya and her Mum, it was possible to look at what they both wanted to achieve. This was basically for Natalie to get back to school without feeling she had to hide or feel scared. They both agreed to attend a restorative conference, if the other girl was agreeable. Natalie was insistent, that the conference take place without both mothers present. Some of Natalie's concerns were that it might make the situation worse and much work was done in talking with Natalie about how Tanya would be approached and that she, like Natalie, would have a choice about attending. It was explained that the emphasis was not upon Tanya getting into more trouble about this - something Natalie did not want - but upon enlisting her involvement in trying to sort the situation out. The common goal would be to enable both girls to go through their school life peaceably.

Natalie agreed and all the assessment boxes for her were GREEN. However the overall restorative assessment was at AMBER, as Tanya had to go through the same restorative preparation.

During the course of the restorative preparation with Tanya, she was told that she would not be "judged" or "blamed" in the conference and that the purpose of it was to try and sort things out together, so that Natalie could return to school and feel safe. This would enable Tanya to get on with her education without getting into any more trouble and also feel able to co-exist with Natalie. Tanya said she had no idea that the reason Natalie had stayed off school was because of her. She was willing to attend a conference. She wanted to put it all behind her and still felt that some teachers thought of her as a bully. She did not like the reputation she was getting. She also felt that there were some other pupils stirring things up for her, so that she might get into further trouble. Although Tanya's mum was involved in the preparation, she was happy for the two girls to be able to sort things out for themselves and she thought both would learn something from it. Tanya also wanted a conference with just herself and Natalie.

At this stage, with the assessments and preparation on both sides having been successfully completed, the conference had a GREEN light to go ahead.

How this case actually looked when it went to conference is documented in Appendix 5.

'I began to understand how to use conflict and contradictions to promote learning'
Myles Horton - The Long Haul

In this chapter we look at:

→ Three levels of Restorative Interventions

→ How do we talk about young people round here?

→ Day to day use of restorative language

→ Some useful phrases for classroom, yard and corridor

→ Why not "why"?

→ Forgiveness

Three levels of Restorative Interventions

Restorative solutions take many forms in schools and care settings. Some can be done routinely, others will take time, commitment and planning to fully implement. Each process can directly involve other pupils/young people in lead roles. Some are more directly focused on restorative outcomes than others.

The three levels at which **restorative interventions** can take place are:

→ Day to day use of restorative language

→ Small / Short conferences

→ Full / Large conferences

Many readers will feel that they already work restoratively and indeed much excellent practice in schools designed to develop personal, social skills and relationships will be restorative.

Working Restoratively is participatory. It is an approach that sees misbehaviour as essentially a violation of people and relationships rather than a violation of rules or establishments or organisations. Restorative Justice, in its widest sense, is defined as "all those affected by an incident or conflict being involved in finding a mutually acceptable way forward". Wrong doers are also recognised as having been affected and therefore involved in finding the way forward. The various processes that can be used to repair harm demand certain skills of facilitators. These include active, empathic listening, impartiality and an ability to empower others to come up with their own solutions to problems. (Robin Tinker, RJ Handbook 2005, Appendix A)

How do we talk about young people round here?

The language of schools

Language is at the heart of working restoratively and cannot be underestimated. Restorative language is not just about what is being said but how people talk to each other; the spirit of the talk and what it embodies. This may lead you to ask some questions about existing patterns of talk in your school setting.

If we were to think of the following frames; blame, punishment, praise and restorative language where would you place the language currently being used in your setting? Within a restorative frame you may become curious about how a child or young person's teacher or other worker communicates with a child or question the messages received from the wider system about young people. How is language used and what does that language potentially do to a child, that is; does it open up new and constructive possibilities for growth and learning or do some ways of speaking close down the potential and opportunities for positive change?

Restorative language is not just about how we talk around the school. It can also involve modelling the talk and therefore how we are acting and responding to different situations that unfold. Pupils will always be watching and listening very closely to how adults deal with incidents of harm or perceived wrongdoing. What exactly are we modelling?

ACTIVITY

Think about how language is used by colleagues around a school or setting you know or work in. How recently have you heard something like:

> She's lazy
>
> He's disruptive
>
> She's a whiner
>
> He's defiant or a troublemaker or a child being directly called stupid girl or a liar?

Or   What's wrong with that kid?

How many times have you noticed the same child getting exclusion after exclusion with nothing gained in terms of positive changes in behaviour? Is this the system getting "stuck" in one response, time after time, with zero effect?

How would you describe the quality of the talk in this school between colleagues? Between pupils? Between staff and pupils? How would you distinguish active listening? Can you sense empathy? Are people taking turns to speak to each other or to others or are they talking over each other? Whose voice gets most heard?

How often do you hear colleagues talking to pupils about their capacities? When a pupil is very hard to manage is anyone naming their gifts, talents, strengths, resilience or interests?

What type of response is invited from the individuals involved? Does this demonstrate respect?

There are many deep-seated beliefs embedded in the way we speak about other people not only in school settings but also in other areas of society. When confronted by difference, disability or social and emotional needs many adults working in schools will focus on what is wrong with an individual, the broken or half empty part.

Deficit talk is influenced by *medical model* views of the world in which the question 'What's wrong?' with that child or adult, dominates our mindset. In this way of thinking school staff can become preoccupied with what is not working, the *deficiency, the impairment, the disorder.* This in turn can lead to actions and strategies designed to remedy, modify, cure or fix.

A more restorative and inclusive orientation focuses on the capacity of individuals and groups. What do they bring? What can we work with? What are the possibilities of goodness? Here we find our language reflects a new preoccupation with *gifts, talents, strengths, resilience and interests* of a pupil as we adopt a more *educational or social model* (Mason and Rieser, 1992) of difference. There is a strong link here with attempts to work and communicate in more person centred, respectful ways with disabled children and adults and those with the most challenging emotional and social needs (O'Brien and O'Brien 2002).

Despite this more positive focus on capacity we will still need to manage situations firmly and constructively when harm occurs but our language will have changed to reflect a restorative vision for relationships both in and out of school.

> Underlying restorative justice is the vision of interconnectedness, which I noted earlier. We are all connected to each other and to the larger world through a web of relationships. When this web is disrupted, we are all affected. The primary elements of restorative justice – harm and need, obligation and participation derive from this vision. (Zehr, 2002)

Day to day use of restorative language

In many schools the typical approach to dealing with misbehaviour involves the adult in asking 3 questions (which are not designed to be genuinely exploratory) to clarify responsibility, establish blame and carry out retributive justice (punishment) in as short a time as possible:

→ What happened?

→ Who is to blame?

→ Which punishment is appropriate?

A restorative intervention, in contrast, involves the adult in genuinely asking those involved the following 5 questions:

→ What happened?

→ What were you thinking?

→ What were you feeling?

→ Who has been affected by what happened?

→ How can we put things right?

Those dealing with very young children may find that the restorative questions suggested will need to be adapted or simplified. Early Years practitioners have found that asking even very young children the question "How can we put things right?" or "How can we make it right?" can have a positive effect. Simple and concrete use of language is essential, taking into account developmental factors and learning needs.

A restorative **dialogue** involves empathic questioning (and listening) with all those concerned, it tries to avoid instant judgement, especially with children who have a history of difficult behaviour. Blame, put downs, sarcastic remarks, labels, criticism, comparisons and diagnoses are all forms of judgement. The Sufi poet Jalaluddin Rumi has written:

Out beyond ideas of wrongdoing and right doing there is a field. I'll meet you there (Rumi, 1207 – 1273)

This is the space the restorative practitioner is trying to open up when working with conflicts between people.

"Stuff" happens in schools. The school community is a messy and often intense world of relationships. We cannot know everything that is going on for each individual child and young person in the school. There is constantly a moving range of meanings and stories informing actions at any one time or in any episode, which occurs between children and young people. It is no surprise, therefore, that people get hurt and that relationships get damaged. Conflict is very real and perhaps more so where pupils are bringing major issues from family and community into the school community.

One consistent piece of feedback from adults who have undergone training in restorative interventions has been that it all sounds "straightforward" or "common sense". However, when they attempt to apply restorative techniques in their work, something else becomes apparent. Some have discovered that it takes a "real effort" not to resort to their familiar patterns of disciplining such as "telling" pupils or "giving advice" especially when they are not getting a desired response from a child or when a child is saying little.

Some useful phrases for classroom, yard and corridor

A number of key words and concepts should find their place in increasingly restorative everyday language around schools and these include the following:

I am not saying you are a good or bad person, but let us look at what has happened and who has been affected by those words/actions. Then we can explore together what needs to happen to put things right and to find a way forward with this.

Tell me in your words what happened?

What does he/she/you/they feel?

What do you think he/she/they might feel?

Who has been affected by those words/actions?

Who has been harmed?

How do you think she feels?

You have just heard how hurt Tara was/affected her family was.

What has changed for you having heard that ?

What are you thinking/feeling now?

How can we make things better?

How can you put things right?

How would you like things between you to be different?

What do you need to do to make things better for Tara and for yourself?

What's the best it can be and how can we achieve that?

What would an agreement look like, who would be doing what?

Can you live with this?

What will you do differently next time?

Who can help you?

Who would be most pleased about what you have achieved here?

How do you think you will feel when you have done what you have agreed to do?

If there's anything in the agreement you are finding hard to keep let us think together what you could do and who is around to help you with that. Who would you like to help you the most?

So....

Starting today, armed with these phrases anyone could begin to be more restorative in responding to things that break down between young people or other adults.

Making Complaints the Restorative Way

Try out some of these questions out when you next need to make a formal complaint to someone.

After stating what has happened using 'I think', 'I feel', 'I and others have been affected in this way'....try asking:

What do you think having heard this?

What can you suggest to put this right?

Can you offer compensation?

What will you do to repair the harm?

What can you suggest that will make me feel more reassured and retain the relationship I have with you and your service?

How will you stick to that agreement?

Colin recently managed to get £50 compensation from Apple Computers for late delivery of a laptop simply by repeatedly asking for reparation!

Why not 'Why?'

One question that is often mistakenly assumed to be restorative is the question, WHY? Nothing is easier than using the question, 'Why?' when dealing with an incident involving one or more pupils. We have taken the question for granted as it is used so frequently around schools. But it is a word that is often interpreted by the receiver as a precursor to blame or as a word to speed things up as the person who has asked the question is assumed to have made up their mind about the incident. Some 'why's' can be experienced as judgemental or confrontational and we therefore question its use and the user's intention.

We would advise that the "why" question is avoided at all costs, if it is our intention to work restoratively. Within a restorative conference, we are looking to use questions that lead to new understandings and to create a space where harm is being repaired. "Why?" becomes redundant. Instead, much care is taken in the choice of alternative questions to use and in our intentions in asking them.

By using restorative language as a matter of course in and around the school a common vocabulary can be introduced. This vocabulary counters the deficit talk, which serves to stigmatise pupils and offers an important alternative by separating the person from the problem. It does not allow children and young people to avoid taking responsibility for their actions. It seeks an acknowledgement of the emotions that might be underpinning some of the behaviours and so helps to move things towards resolution.

Restorative solutions focus on the impact of particular actions, how they have affected another/others and what can be done to help restore the relationship. By its very nature therefore restorative, "talk" has a future focus. The language is inclusive, community orientated and person centred.

Forgiveness

When did you last hear the words 'Can you forgive me?' or 'You are forgiven?' We have found over the course of many training sessions that almost any adult group will list forgiveness as something they felt they needed if they had harmed someone by their actions or words. So why is forgiveness rarely mentioned in school policy documentation and never in Behaviour Policies?

The word forgiveness can often be loathed by victims who feel they should not have to do the work involved in forgiving without the person who harmed them fully taking responsibility for their actions. Yet for forgiveness to take place both must give up their positions as victim and offender. A complete turn around is needed. The offender will need to truly take responsibility for their actions and rationalisations and act differently in the future and the victim must be free enough of anger and resentment to have the power to speak and forgive. What an amazing domino effect of forgiveness might be achieved. (Janet Handy, 2005)

We are reaching for the possibility of forgiveness in this new restorative language of relationships. This is the new, but ancient 'f' word. We reach here for a timeless value. Forgiveness can be requested and can be offered. Our every day language needs to embrace this strong restorative concept. Can you picture adults forgiving each other publicly, adults asking pupils to forgive them and actively forgiving pupils? This is the challenge.

Forgiveness does not mean ignoring what has been done or putting a false label on an evil act. It means, rather, that the evil act no longer remains as a barrier to the relationship. Forgiveness is a catalyst creating the atmosphere necessary for a fresh start and a new beginning. It is the lifting of a burden or the cancelling of a debt.
(Martin Luther King, 1963)

'Problems are my friends' Tom Peters

In this chapter we will describe:

→ What a short conference is

→ A Short Restorative Conference Format

When serious incidents of harm or damage occur in a school setting, most staff and families will expect something to be 'done', a formal response from the school management. This is where a Short Restorative Conference or a Full Restorative Conference can be used. The school will need to ask itself the following questions:

Has harm been done? Is there a need to repair the harm? Do we have the time to make this investment in our school community? Can we afford not to? (Thoresby, 2003)

A Short Conference

A "Short" Restorative Conference usually involves at least three people - the adult who is dealing with the incident and the two children or young people involved. Each participant is encouraged to tell what has happened, what they were thinking and feeling at the time, who was affected and then to identify the harm that has been done. Each is invited to say what they think should be done to repair the harm or make things right.

This approach is suitable for most minor incidents, conflicts and disputes where parents/carers do not need to be involved. These short conferences can sometimes be run "on the spot" or at little notice and a quiet room is preferable - somewhere you can place chairs in a circle without a table as a barrier. We have been pressed to run short conferences during lesson time in quiet parts of the dining hall, in the library or in unused classrooms but this is far from ideal, as there are always distractions and potential interruptions.

Short Conference Summary Script

The script represents a plan, a 'mud map', to assist you manage the process of the conference (Thoresby, 2003)

Following a script can make sense when you are starting out or until you are familiar with the format and are confident enough to make it your own.

At the Conference Venue

It is important to ensure privacy and, if possible, keep the victim and offender separate before the conference begins. The facilitator should meet and greet both pupils seating the victim and offenders either side of his or her self.

The Conference Format
(Adapted from Tinker et al, 2006)

This is a basic conference format. Similar questions are asked to each person present to ensure fairness. Given the different positions held there will be a slight variation in the questions asked of each participant and you will need to trust your instincts and sensitivity to judge when and how to do this. Be flexible.

1. Introductions: Introduce whoever present.

2. Welcome: Thank both pupils for coming and stress that they have agreed to come. To show appreciation that they have begun the process and want things to be different, it is appropriate to congratulate individuals for choosing to attend. In some settings such as the Hammersmith and Fulham pilot schools, children and young people prefer to include a few basic ground rules at the beginning of the conference and this option will be discussed further in the next chapter.

The facilitator needs to appear neutral, but warm and encouraging as they open up this meeting. The situation needs to be safe and well managed. A certain business like professionalism needs to be clear in the demeanour of the facilitator from the outset. The meeting is going to be effectively chaired.

3. State the purpose of the conference:

We are here today to focus on the incident which happened on _____ between A _____ (person who harmed) and B _____ (person harmed). A___has admitted his/her part in the incident. We are not here today to take sides or decide who is right or wrong, good or bad but to look in detail at what happened and how B___was affected by that. We will look into how that harm can be repaired and hopefully draw up an agreement together, which will set out how things can

be put right. Both of you will have the opportunity to have your say and be listened to. I will be asking you questions in turn.

This may have to be reworded for some pupils. The facilitator needs to ensure that all present have understood what has been said. The facilitator must take care to avoid any suggestion of blame, judgement, or anger in their nonverbal communications as well as in what they are saying aloud.

4. Questions to A_____:

What happened?
What were you thinking?
How did you feel?
What have your thoughts been since that time?
Who has been affected by your actions?

5. Questions to B_____:

What happened?
What were you thinking?
How did you feel?
What has been the hardest thing for you?
Who else has been affected by what happened?

6. Question to A_____:

You have just heard how B_____ has been affected by what you did and how what you did has caused harm. Is there anything you would like to say?

7. A's_____ response:

Alternatively in the case where both parties have been responsible for causing harm to the other we might say to A and B:

We have heard what each of you have had to say, tell me what you are feeling now?

8. Question to A_____:

What can you do to put things right?

9. Variations to this question:

What do you need (is there anything you can do) to do to put things right?
Is there anything more you want to say?

10. A_____(offers reparation)

This question is difficult for some children and young people. Allow them time to come up with something. If the facilitator judges that the child or young person is really struggling, he or she may wish to invite some ideas from the other young person or to ask a question like: **What do you think B____ might need to feel safe with you?** *Tentatively offering some ideas and suggestions may be appropriate for those children who continue to struggle, in order to ensure that a range of options are offered. Also it is crucial that you check out that what they then choose has some meaning to them. The young person can then translate these into their own words and say how they will carry them out i.e. days, times etc. What is offered must be realistic and achievable.*

The facilitator could ask further questions to find out who might be able to support and assist the young person in honouring the commitment. A useful question at this stage might be: **Is there anyone else who can support you in this?**

11. Question to B_____:

How do you feel about that offer?

Continue dialogue until a satisfactory resolution is achieved.

12. Question to A_____:

On (date) **you made the choice to** (summarise the incident) **and today you have made another choice and have agreed to** (summarise reparation offered). **Which choice do you feel better about?**

13. Question to B_____:

You have heard _____ say how his/her behaviour has caused harm and what he/she will do to put this right. How do you feel now?

14. Pupils draw up the agreement.
Both sign it.
Agree to meet again to review how things are going and whether the Agreement has been adhered to in a reconvened conference.
Date this.

The process of completing the Agreement and signing can be a time of informal reconnecting for the involved pupils. The facilitator is wise to give them some space as they do this.

15. Questions to A_____:

You have said that you have taken responsibility for what you did and that you are going to put things right by: (sum up agreement)

How do you feel now?

How will (these people) feel if you do not keep to the agreement?

How will B feel if you keep to the agreement?

How will you feel if you keep to the agreement?

How will I feel if you break the agreement?

How will I feel if you keep the agreement?

At this stage you might want to say something about the follow up meeting and the form that will take. Sometimes this might be informal but for more serious cases setting a time to check how the agreements are going is important. You may wish to repeat some of these questions to B.

16. Facilitator:

Congratulates A_____ and B_____ on making positive choices and both for listening to each other. Emphasise B___'s courage for facing A___.
Thanks pupils for coming.

17. Post Conference Tasks:

Staff information sheet completed and posted on notice board.

Conference record sheet completed - Copies in each pupil's files.

Agreements photocopied - originals to pupils.
                                   - copy to each pupil's file.

18. Evaluation sheets (if used):

A copy for A___ and B_____ and for involved school staff.

‘What the best and wisest parent wants for his own child, that must be what the community wants for all its children’ John Dewey

In this chapter we will describe:

→ Guiding principles of the full restorative conference

→ Preparation before the full conference

→ A New Zealand Conference Process Outline

→ A five stage model of managing a full conference with/without a script

→ A staged approach with some suggested script

→ Opening stage: welcome, introductions, purpose, context, ground rules, time out

→ Exploration stage

→ Moving on stage: what needs to happen now and in the future to restore things?

→ Negotiating agreements stage: apology, looking ahead and dialogue

→ Closure stage

Guiding principles of the full restorative conference (a recap)

Restorative justice is a process to involve, to the greatest extent possible, those who have a stake in a specific offence and to collectively identify and address harms, needs, and obligations, in order to heal and put things as right as possible. (Zehr, 2003)

Restorative justice works according to the premise that crime and conflict inflict harm and that individuals must accept responsibility for repairing that harm. Conflict is viewed as an opportunity for a community to learn and grow and for those involved to have their needs addressed. For this reason, the needs of all those affected by the harm are central in any restorative process. Howard Zehr emphasises the importance of placing key stakeholders at the forefront of the process and shaping of the resolution.

When serious harm has occurred and there is enough imagination and commitment around to wish to avoid an exclusion or long-term segregation from mainstream education, then a full conference may be considered appropriate. This involves gathering together all the key stakeholders and those most affected by what has happened. Facilitation of full conferences is clearly more challenging but the potential payoffs are immense.

Preparation before the full conference

Before the meeting you will need to be clear on the following:

→ What exactly happened?

→ Who was involved?

→ What has happened since?

→ Is it clear who did what?

The conference must not be too soon or too long after the event and most practitioners agree that around 5 days after an incident is about right. This does not rule out conferencing an issue that has been going on for months or even years.

The key preparatory stages are as follows:

1. Establish facts and decide who will attend

→ Who was most affected by what happened?

→ Who are the key stakeholders in this being resolved?

Put simply, this community consists of those who did it and those who had it done to them. (Thoresby, 2003)

All participants should have some role or stake in the process and could include:

→ "The Victim" plus their family or carers and friends

→ "The Offender" with supporters such as family and friends

→ Witnesses

→ School staff

→ Support Services who are involved already

→ Governors

The incident may have created a breakdown in pupil friendship groups. The school or local community may be deeply hurt or divided over what has happened. The right people must be there if the offender and victim are to be included back into their educational and caring communities.

Relationships need to be repaired. Those most in need of repair need to be present at the conference. (Thoresby, 2005)

You may have to actively create a circle of support around either "victim" or (more likely) "offender". Deliberately reach out to people and invite their involvement building on any connections the young person already has with those around them.

Who loves this pupil?

When creating a circle of support around either a victim or someone who has caused harm you might be left wondering which pupils and adults to get involved. The young person may be unpopular, regularly rejected, actively disliked or worse. Now could be a good time to ask Herb Lovett's (1996) famous question **'Who loves this person?'** Herb spent his professional life working with segregated and excluded adults with challenging behaviour in the United States. These were adults who had been locked up because of their behaviour. In his excellent book 'Learning to Listen' he raises this question as one of the most important to be asked when working around individuals with challenging behaviour. We all share a need to be accepted and to belong however we behave. He argued that whatever the answer is, that is where you will need to begin the work! So for the child for whom the answer to this question is 'no one loves them' then relationship building work needs to begin in earnest. For the pupil for whom the answer involves a grandmother who lives miles away, then it is she who must be reached out to somehow.

2. Interview key participants before the conference

The importance of the preparation interviews cannot be overstated, as it will be at this stage that you will find whether or not the conference can go ahead. There may be all sorts of emotions still evident for some participants and you will be checking out these and preparing people for how these feelings might be contained safely within the conference.

→ **How are you feeling about being part of this conference?**

→ **You will be asked to talk about what happened and what you have been feeling and thinking since. What do you think you will say? How can we make this feel safe for you?**

→ **We will need to expressing our feelings without blaming anyone, will you be able to manage this OK? Can we support you in any way with this?**

The conference is not the place for debating details of the incident. The interviews should clarify and confirm stories and responsibilities. The facilitator needs no big surprises on new developments in the conference itself. Rehearse all the questions that will be raised at the conference. You may have to convince parents or staff to put on hold other actions or disciplinary procedures until after the conference.

For example, Aaron aged 14, was discovered as the one responsible for continuously putting rubbish into another pupil's bag and had been described as a "bully" by his Head of Year. From this pupil's point of view he thought that he was the one who "always got blame". No one was prepared to listen to what he had to say and "no one could see fully where he was coming from". The staff were keen to give him a fixed-term exclusion for his behaviour but were convinced to hold on until after what turned out to be a very successful conference before they decided on this.

3. Arrange a time, venue and refreshments / hospitality

Privacy and a place where there are unlikely to be interruptions are key conditions for a successful conference. Sometimes a completely neutral venue can help, or a venue that is not already loaded with history for either child/young person. So avoiding school settings for some situations can be helpful. Venues such as community centres, church halls or meeting rooms, or even upstairs in a local pub are worth exploring. Refreshments are also crucial to setting the right tone for the meeting. They are powerful signals of welcome and inclusion.

If you have 10-15 people likely to participate allow 2 hours for the conference. Be flexible and prepared to negotiate as you attempt to find a time that all can attend. This will be a major challenge. Try going for before school, late afternoon or evenings to maximise attendance.

Refreshments provided at the end of the meeting can allow for some friendly mixing between those present, where the work done in the conference can continue! There is nothing like eating and drinking with others to create a sense of connection, belonging and to confirm resolution.

4. Create a seating plan

Many workers and writers on restorative justice have detailed views on seating plans (See for instance Thoresby, 2003). There is an important balance to be sought within the room that avoids too much physical support/presence being around either the victim or the offender. The circle is helpful as it suggests connection. The room layout must not suggest confrontation so try to minimise any feeling or appearance of 'sides'. The facilitator's position is central and they must be visible to all parties.

5. Anticipate likely tensions and relationship issues

Talk to people who know the participants. Check out the dynamics between those who will be present. Has the incident occurred in the middle of a long-standing feud between two families or even as part of a gang culture within the community? How are people likely to behave? What do you need to do to keep it safe? Some situations have called for the presence of someone who is mutually respected by both parties. What else will help reassure those present? Perhaps one of the most important aspects of the preparation is for each of the participants to develop a trust in the process, and the facilitator.

6. Consider communication needs

Do you need an interpreter? If English is a second language for any of the participants this will be crucial. Check what the first language of pupils' parents is and arrange for an interpreter if necessary. It is equally important to spend some time with the interpreter explaining the process and the aims of the conference and to establish their capacity to remain neutral. If anyone is deaf, they may well need a signer. Do either the victim or offender need a 'communication ally' because of his or her own communication support requirements? A young person with autism, or with the label of severe learning or communication difficulties might well need such an ally.

The communication ally is someone ... making sure the situation is structured so that the person is fully informed, heard and respected throughout the proceedings. ...(they) use their fluency privilege on behalf of people who experience limited or impaired ability to communicate fluently. (Shevin, 2002)

Consider creating a graphic record of the whole conference process using a wall sized piece of paper, coloured pens and a graphic facilitator (Inclusive Solutions 2008: unpublished work in progress).

7. Consider cultural needs

Be aware of cultural differences and the meaning that different cultures may give to parts of the restorative process. To be culturally aware and sensitive we must not take anything for granted and this includes introductions. This is something that can be checked out at the preparation stage; whether people want to introduce themselves and in what way. Your focus is on ensuring respect for everyone taking part. There may be very different gender expectations in some cultures, which there will need to be some sensitivity around. It may be less acceptable in some cultures to talk in public about feelings. The facilitator must ensure that families or the child/young person involved are not made to feel needlessly uncomfortable.

8. Consider how you will manage participants arrival

It is important to attend carefully to the initial contact, as this will set the scene. This means giving thought to how you will greet the participants on arrival, and where they will sit/wait. It can be a time of anxiety, tension, discomfort, therefore allow each group their own separate waiting space to avoid any unhelpful exchanges. You may have to use the conference room itself and use can be made of classrooms or office space if available. It is always a good idea to have others around to help with the welcome and greetings. Unexpected newcomers may turn up and need to be talked to individually and prepared. Someone will need to show people where the amenities are. The aim is to get the conference started at the agreed time.

9. Be organised and methodical

Having the clear restorative framework in mind, keeping the pace but not rushing anyone will help to ensure that people get heard. The process of the meeting is as important as what gets said and how. Practical tools in your restorative tool kit include:

- Remember you have a structured step by step process with set questions to help guide you and contain the dialogue

- Some facilitators like to have a pen, paper and script to hand even if it is not used other like to have someone else present who will keep a live and large graphic record of what is being said

- A script is useful as a quick reference back or to help refocus when the discussion has gone off track or when you are thrown out of sequence. Be prepared to bring the focus back to the purpose of the meeting

- A seating plan, names, blank agreements and other paperwork should be ready

Showing this level of organisation may feel very containing especially at the outset when people do not really know each other and may be ill at ease.

Be prepared at times for the focus to veer off on a tangent. At these times you need to hear what has been said but also keep the boundaries of the meeting clear for all present. You may need to chair the meeting with firm discipline.

10. Stay flexible

Flexibility is about noticing and giving space to those conversations that look as if they are going to move things on. The most effective conferences have created a truly restorative ethos marked by a spontaneous flow and dialogue between people. Many have found that towards the later part of a conference, when the focus moves to needs, actions, agreements and who can support these, there is often more open and easier dialogue.

Compare the full conference outline used in New Zealand with Maori communities with the process we are exploring in the UK context.

Conference Process Outline

Before arriving at a conference each person has had a chance to be invited to join in, and to understand how the conference will work and what its goals are. The importance of engaging with people before the conference cannot be overstated.

1.　As appropriate, a conference will begin with a formal welcome, prayers and greetings.

2.　"The problem is the problem, the person is not the problem" goes on the board or is spoken about.

3.　What are you hoping to see happen in this hui (conference style gathering)? Each person has a chance to speak.

4.　What is the problem that has brought us here? People tell their own versions.

5.　What are the effects of that problem on all present (and others)?

6.　What times, places and relationships do we know of where the problem is not present?

7.　What new description of the people involved becomes clear as we look at the times and places where the problem is not present?

8.　If there have been people / things harmed by the problem, what is it that you need to happen to see amends being made?

9.　How does what we have spoken about and seen in the alternative descriptions help us plan to overcome the problem? People contribute ideas and offers of resources that help overcome the problem.

10.　Does that plan meet the needs of anyone harmed by the problem?

11.　People are given responsibility to carry each part of the plan forward. Any follow up is planned for.

12.　Karakia (prayers) and thanks. Hospitality may be offered.

University of Waikatu, New Zealand:
Restorative Practices Development Team (2003)

A five-stage model of managing a conference with or without a script

A model for working without a script proceeds as follows:

1. Welcome and Opening Stage

Welcomes, introductions, creating a context for listening, talking, agreeing ground rules, setting the context of the conference and time out.

2. Exploration Stage (Past/Present)

Around the incident(s) what happened then (before) who affected, what's happened since. Each participant will be asked in turn the appropriate questions before moving onto the next stage.

3. Moving On Stage (Present/Future)

In setting the foundations for moving on there is a need to check what people need now and next to restore things.

4. Negotiating Agreements Stage

This is a negotiating process whereby pupils and participants are encouraged to take the lead. (Pupils can do this together on their own and bring back to share if they choose).

5. Closure Stage

At this stage there is a drawing together of what has been achieved by everyone in the meeting. Part of the closing phase will include reminders of follow up actions.

A staged approach with some suggested script

Stage One   Welcoming and Opening Stage

Welcomes, introductions, setting the context and creating a context for listening, talking, safety and a sense of belonging are all features of this stage.

Preparing for this opening stage is important and sets the tone for what follows. It is often the stage where people are a bit nervous, anxious, and uncomfortable about being there. The scene can literally be set in that first part and forms the basis of the dialogue that is to follow.

1. Welcome

One example of full conference script:

Welcome and thank you for choosing to give up your own time to come here today to work through this together in a way that will allow both pupil A and pupil B to continue safely and peaceably in this school. It would be helpful if we could all go round the circle and say who we are and what brings each of us here today, and who each person is in relation to each of the pupils *(use names here).*

Here you can judge whether it would be helpful for you to start things off:

> My name is……..and my role is to coordinate the conference and to ensure that everyone has a say. I am not here to take sides or to make any judgements about anybody but to help to move things on in a way that is agreeable to everyone.

2. Names

Do not assume people know each other's names and do not take introductions for granted, even if the pupils involved have been in the same class for a number of years. By asking them to say their name and checking how they would like to be referred to during this conference you demonstrate respectful interaction. Name badges can help this too. The issue of respecting names becomes important, if there has been derogatory name calling/verbal abuse/threats and intimidation involved. Names are important.

3. Creating Context

When everyone has spoken or found some way to communicate, it can be good to round up with:

> We are here together to hear what has happened but in a way that might help us to understand a bit more and in a different way what it was like for each person here
>
> We want also to hear how everyone has been affected and to see how we can make things better and move forward.

A statement reiterating the purpose of the conference may help clarify and orientate the group's focus towards the process. For example:

> We are not here to make judgements or to say anyone is a good or bad person. We are here to look at what happened from everyone's position, to see how everyone has been affected and how this might be put right so that everyone can move on assured that it will not happen again. Each person will have a

chance to have their say and all we would ask is to be respectful of each other and to listen when the other person is telling their story and how they felt. We hope by the end of the meeting we will see what people need in order to move on and that agreements can be reached. We will be exploring how we might help these two young people (names) keep to their agreements.

Or still simpler:

We are not here to take sides, or to judge anyone. We are going to really listen to everyone here today and will try to find a way forward.

4. Agree Ground Rules

Ground rules or promises need to be established at this early stage of being together. It is helpful to ask the group for their agreement to keep the content of the meeting in the room. Be clear about the limits to confidentiality if it emerges that anyone has been or might be at risk.

Typical set of ground rules:

→ Confidential unless someone discloses being hurt or in danger

→ Mutual Respect

→ One person speaking at a time

→ No preaching at each other

Let the group know it will be necessary to share outcomes and agreements reached today with key members of staff so that they can help the young people stick to their agreements.

5. Set the Context

In the case of one clear incident such as a fight or a particular assault that occurred, set that context. State clearly the incident the conference will focus upon, where, when, involving whom (names).

For example, in a reintegration conference, you might be stating that (name) will be returning to school after a ten day exclusion for punching (name) in the face.

As we know in schools there may not be a clear-cut "victim" and "perpetrator" and there can be often a longstanding history of various tensions and conflict between the young people involved. In this case you will be adapting your introduction. In this example three pupils were involved on either side of the conflict:

We will be looking at the fight which took place between (name each pupil), on...., at.......This is the most recent of a series of events which have been erupting this term and we want to understand how it got to this stage. We are not here to say that anyone is a good or bad person or to take sides but to explore how people view their own involvement in what happened, what harm has been caused and who has been affected by this. We hope to look at how things can be repaired and to arrive at some common ground and agreements about how to continue together at school in a peaceable way.

6. Time Out

Anyone has the right to leave and no longer participate but clarify that school staff will have to decide what happens next if this involves key participants. Check that everyone is OK with that.

> At any stage in the meeting you may feel you have to leave. Please feel free to return as soon as you can.

Or…

> If anyone wishes to leave the room at any stage for a few moments that is ok and we will endeavour to find a member of staff to sit with them.

Stage Two Exploration Stage (Past/Present)

1. Exploring the incident

- → What happened?
- → What happened before?
- → Who has been affected?
- → What's happened since?

Most of the texts on restorative conferencing state, *"that the order in which people have been invited to tell their stories is critical. Wrongdoers first, then their supporters, followed by the victim and their parents or caregivers and their supporters."* (Thorsborne and Vinegrad, 2002)

The type of questions asked and the way they are asked are crucial to how the meeting will proceed. Fair, even and open questions to each participant without bias is important. A useful guideline is to seek clarification where there is confusion and explore further where significant things seem to have been glossed over.

Remember you are not trying to look for evidence or proof, nor are you trying to get people to 'explain themselves'.

Examples of questions that may be asked here are:

> To help us gain a greater understanding of what occurred, who was affected and how, could you, in your own words, describe what happened?

(Drawing out where, when, who else was around and what you did in relation to them, what was said, actions and responses.)

It will be useful for facilitators to have extra questions available to help the young person tell his or her story. Many young people may find it quite daunting to talk in a larger group. It is important not to assume that we know the meaning of behaviours or gestures in the room; a young person might giggle at times, not because they want to be disrespectful but because they feel very nervous in the conference situation. One teacher, who had participated in a conference about one pupil who had explicitly hurt another pupil, was surprised how her perception switched during the conference. She initially interpreted the reluctance of this pupil to tell their side of the story as confirming her image of this boy as "a bully". In fact, with the help of his mother, the boy explained that he deeply regretted his actions, felt very ashamed of what he had done and even shared that he had fretted about the conference since it had come to light and had had sleepless nights. This gave the teacher a completely different perception of this boy's inner world. She could no longer simply view him simply as a self styled 'hard man' or unfeeling bully.

It is crucial to the process that the facilitator remain curious at all times and resists the urge to interpret what is happening. However, some gentle prompts may help the story unfold:

What happened next?

And then?

Can you say a bit more about that?

And what led up to this?

How far do we need to go?

Is it ok to go back a bit, can you remember what was happening before you ran out of the class?

Thinking and feeling questions are deliberately woven into the questioning:

What were you thinking/feeling at the time?

What was going on inside for you when you did that?

How did you come to take that action and not another?

What were the other options you had at that time?

How were you thinking/feeling at that particular moment? (e.g. when you were striking a blow, or saying something insulting).

Facilitators may need to probe for the detail, such as:

How did you hit him/her (with open hand, clenched fist)?

You can be creative in the way you ask these questions for example:

What were your fists saying?

Are you able to say here what was going on for you at that time (thoughts/feelings)?

At what point did you manage/decide to stop?

Who do you think was affected by this?

Who else?

At the time? Since?

In what ways?

Be sensitive to young people, who may find these questions difficult. The process itself will create opportunities for them to reflect.

If it seems like the young person is struggling at any stage it can be helpful to ask:

How are you feeling now?

To prepare the young person to move towards the next stage of exploring the harm done in more detail, a useful question is:

What have you thought about since this happened? And now?

In cases where there is clearly a pupil who has been harmed this marks a punctuation point and it is time to explore the harm in some depth.

The tone and questions for the person who has been harmed would be very similar to those already used.

Types of questions to the person who has been harmed include:

From your position at that time what happened?

What were you thinking/feeling?

What was the most difficult part of that?

What has it been like for you coming to school since?

How has what happened affected you?

What has been the personal cost to you?

What has been the hardest thing for you since?

How have you managed?

How did your family/friends/teachers (choose whoever is appropriate in the

context) feel/respond when they found out about the incident?

How have they been affected?

There may be other stories about and effects that you will have heard about in your preparation with this young person such as other relationships changing or things being different for them at home or school. You need to draw these out.

What has been different for you at home/school?

How has this changed things with friends/family?

Be aware of the age, maturity, learning and language skills of the child/young person and change your language to fit these needs. If they are finding it difficult to give a response at this stage, give them time but do not push for a response. The important thing is that your questions may facilitate reflections from others about the wider impact of the incident. The child's parent/carer/supporter in particular may wish to expand further on this impact.

2. Anger and Distress

There may be times in the telling of their stories when people closest to the events may become distressed or angry. This needs to be responded to by the facilitator. Helping them to acknowledge and name some of their anger and distress may be helpful.

Useful questions here are:

How are you feeling now?

What are the key things here for you?

What are the main aspects of this for you?

What has been the worst thing in all of this for you?

It may be that they have questions they want to ask or that they have residual fears or worries.

Are there any questions that you may have or anything you are wondering about?

Most importantly in this stage remember to enable the young person to voice some of the emotional components as well as practical components of the harm. There may be various stresses and worries being experienced. Very often it is the expression of these vulnerabilities that has the most powerful impact on those present. This is true whether it is done by the young person who inflicted the harm or by the young person on the receiving end. Either way this may be the human connection that can light up the conference.

3. Questions to supporters of the person harmed

Supporters usually include parents/carers, friends/colleagues of the young person who has been harmed. We have found it vital to ask questions that enable the supporters to express the emotional impact of the incident on them. Much of this may be shown outwardly in anger or high anxiety. They may feel quite helpless in the face of the hurt experienced by their child. Uncles and Aunts can be a resource here. For example, when a mother came to a conference with her 15 year old she felt unable to talk "without getting into a state about it". She did agree to sit and listen and we invited the Aunt to be mum's spokesperson.

How did you come to hear about the incident?

What were you thinking/feeling?

How did you see the effect of this on your son/daughter?

What was that like for you as a parent/friend/colleague ?

What's been the hardest thing since?

Here you may be trying to draw out any changes they may have noticed or struggles they may be having as a result.

> **And the main issues?**

4. Questions to the supporters of the person who has done the harm

Similarly this group is made up of parents/carers, friends, colleagues as a group who are most closely connected to the young person, they are vitally important to the process and its impact on the young person.

There may also be feelings of shame, disappointment, disbelief and upset around especially after hearing what has been said. It is helpful therefore to acknowledge this and to be appreciative of their waiting and listening.

> **What has it been like for you listening to this (thoughts/feelings)?**
>
> **What was it like when you heard about what happened?**
>
> **How did you feel and how did you react?**
>
> **What have things been like since for you?**
>
> **How has this affected you?**
>
> **What are things like now between you all?**

5. Reflections on Stage 2 of Facilitation Process

Here we might hear about various sanctions that have been put in place as a result of the incident such as being grounded, pocket money stopped and so on. Also relationships at home may have become fraught. We have found, in the cases where parents are very critical of their son/daughter, that it is important to focus back on the child's courage in being there and trying with everyone to sort things out. This might be an opportunity to invite parents and carers to notice that the young person is here and is addressing a difficult issue. By this type of immediate feedback and spotlighting what the young person is doing well you can model how to notice the positive behaviours you want to reinforce in that young person. Look for questions that will draw out descriptions of other, more positive aspects of the young person in their relationship or look to others in the room to offer some positive feedback.

Alternatively, if the response to these questions is complete surprise that their child has acted so out of character, use this as an opening to draw out the parts which have made this one incident an exception rather than the young person feeling defined by the one harmful act.

It is not the role of the facilitator to step into a defending role of the school or to give opinions. A key element is to remain neutral and to ensure everyone has a say and gets heard.

6. Defensiveness

There may be times when you sense that a supporter is siding heavily with the young person, who has done the hurtful action. There can be many beliefs that make people act this way.

→ Feeling that they are being judged

→ They have failed as a parent

→ Viewing the education system as punitive/authoritarian, which leads to a need to defend their child

→ Blaming the school and how they have responded. For example, we have heard in conferences parents/carers say: " We should have been notified earlier." "That teacher is always having a go at my son/daughter", " How has the school let this get out of all proportion, why wasn't it nipped in the bud?"

This may be an indication that the relationship between school and parent/carer may need to be repaired. Use non-threatening questions, which invite them to take a different position, and link to both what the school and parent wants and what pupils might need.

What sort of behaviour would you like to be assured of to ensure that your son/daughter is safe in school?

And what do you think now in relation to the boy/girl's actions towards your son/daughter?

7. Watch the dynamics

Be aware and attentive to both the dynamics and the process (as well as the content). Many teachers will already be very adept at this. Be prepared for the person who talks too much and tries to dominate and the person who says very little. You will need all your interpersonal skills and facilitation strategies at the ready. So, for instance, you may need to "thank" someone for their input and ask them to "hold onto some of those important issues while we hear from…."

Stage Three   Moving on Now and in the Future

This stage addresses moving from the context of the conference to the real world life outside where the children will be co-existing without adults being around at all times.

In laying the foundations for moving on, you need to check that everything has been sufficiently covered. This moves the conference on to what people need (now) and what needs to happen next to restore things?

Suggested Script for Stage 3 Moving on:

To the person causing the harm:

>**Is there anything else you would like to say now having heard about those affected and the harm caused?**
>
>**What do you think? .... might need now to feel safe/ok around the school?**

To person who has been harmed:

>**What is the most important thing to happen for you right now?**
>
>**What might .... do to help/to repair the harm?**

Some other variations on these questions:

>**Is there anything we need to talk through before we move on?**
>
>**Are there any questions at this stage that need to be asked before moving forward?**

A question to the young person who has been harmed and their supporters might be:

>**What are you hoping might happen now?**

This can then be put to the other side.

Now might also be a good time to give some space to the young person who has done the harm so that they can comment and reflect upon what they have done and about what they have heard about how others have been affected.

>**Is there anything you would like to say to…... or anyone else?**
>
>**What do you think might be helpful for…... to hear at this stage, what do you think they might need?**

Be aware of the times when some encouragement or other positive feedback may be required. Offer an appreciation of listening, or that an individual is able to hold a different view whilst respecting the view of someone else.

Stage Four   Negotiating Agreements

In this stage an Agreement will be negotiated that will be considered acceptable to all the key participants. Consensus will be pursued, or at least an arrangement that all can **live with**.

There will be a negotiating process whereby pupils and participants are increasingly encouraged to take the lead. In some situations pupils can even create an agreement together, independently and bring it back to the conference to share if they choose.

1. The Issue of Apologies

Apologies are not always forthcoming in the meeting and must not be forced, even though for many adults it is a desired outcome. Often apologies do happen but outside of the conference room or quite quietly while agreements are being written. 'Sorry' may be a word that is hard for many young people to use or no one has ever said this to the young person before. If 'sorry' happens in a private moment the facilitator, who might be left feeling concerned that an apology was not acknowledged within the structure of the conference, may not know it. However, for many young people it is more meaningful to say sorry in a space where they feel more comfortable. This is in contrast to some of the authoritative responses of "you've got to say sorry" which are likely to elicit only half-hearted apologies.

2. Looking Ahead

Starting with the person who has been harmed some useful questions might be:

What is the most important thing to happen for you right now?

What might… do to help with that? (or repair the harm).

What would you like to see happen from this meeting today?

What do you need to hear from…(agree to) to assure you it will not happen again?

The harmed young person is more often able to say what they do not want to happen. "I don't want to be cussed" or "I don't want to be given a dirty look every time I walk into class", "I don't want ……to spread rumours about me", or I don't want those text messages sent to me'. It is important to hear this and then try to reframe it into what they do want to happen.

You could use an adaptation of "the miracle question" (De Shazer 1985) or the 'dream' question used in person centred planning (Falvey, Pearpoint and Forrest, 1994). In a non-threatening and accessible way allow the person harmed to think about what needs to change. What do they dream of for themselves?

> **If you were to imagine that a miracle had happened and this was all sorted exactly how you wanted it to be. When you woke up what would you notice that proved that this miracle had happened?**

> **If everything was working well, your life was on track for you, what would you dream that it might look like? What would be different? How would you be feeling?**

There is an art in the framing and timing of the miracle question. Its value is that it can elicit so much information about what needs to change in the relationships between people.

Others can be encouraged to share their responses on behalf of the person harmed too.

3. Making Reparation

It is in stage 3 that there is more frequent back and forth questions to both sides and generally more discussion between the parties. You should be encouraging the young person who has done the harm (and supporters) to respond.

You can choose here to go round one by one taking suggestions from all participants. Bear in mind that the most important key wishes and needs are those of the persons who have been directly affected. All supporters can be encouraged to support the young people on each side in their needs and agreements they make together.

To the person who has done the harm (and their supporters):

> **What do you think?**
>
> **How might you begin to put things right/make amends/repair the harm?**
>
> **How reasonable/fair does that sound?**
>
> **What could you agree to do to help.....feel safe?**

To supporters:

> **How might ......do something that might repair things with...?**
> **What might that be?**

Establishing what is agreeable, fair, and realistic are key here; it is not about shame, blame or public humiliation but about giving to what they can actively do, say or agree to.

This could be opened to supporters from both sides by asking:

> **Who in the room can help with this?**

Ideally it is a time when the resources in the room can be really drawn upon and support structures put in place for those children and young people who need them.
It may also be an opportunity for the school to consider their structures, policies and practices and to think about who is around who can help these young people in keeping to the agreements made. A question to encourage consideration around this might be:

Is there something you would like to help support that?

In a case where there is not a fit between what is being asked and what the other party feels they can agree on, it is important to help the whole group refocus on what they are trying to achieve and the purpose of the meeting. Naming what is happening followed by a question might help to open the flow again. For example:

We seem to have reached a bit of an impasse and both those things are important to each side. How can we move beyond that?

What is the most important thing you wanted to get out of this meeting today?

Or (to both sides):

If there was one thing that you wanted young person (1)………and young person (2)………to take/learn from this today what would that be?

Sometimes it is the adults in the room who have an agenda. This can be parents/carers or school staff and other professionals. It is necessary to help shift the focus back on the relationship between the children/young people and how they can be supported in being in school together.

What can you agree on that they/she/he can do to put things right?

4. The Agreements

Agreements must be *"realistically achievable and written in language which is concrete and easily understood."* (Thorsborne & Vinegrad, 2002 p.31).

The agreements should detail each item that is agreed upon, such as:

I will meet ……at the school gate and walk her into school

I agree to be civil whenever I come across ….. at school - no dirty looks or cracking jokes as she walks by

A gentle reminder about confidentiality and how they might keep it might be useful here.

It is advisable to write down word for word what has been said and to read back the list of actions to the group. In some conferencing models, the agreements are given out to the young person/people to write as a "contract" agreement with signature to then pass to each participant to sign. (See Appendix 1)

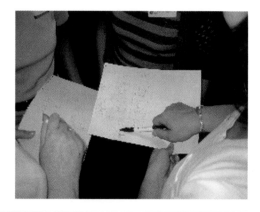

You may ask here:

> **Are you ready to write down in your own words what you will agree to do?**

And more generally:

> **Who is around to help you stick to your agreements?**

You may wish to ask some "what if?" questions to get them thinking ahead about useful strategies for the future and support they might need when they are struggling to keep to the agreement.

The more traditional model suggests that the facilitator records the agreement making that explicit, perhaps reading it aloud as it is written. Ask for a signature and explain that each person will be given a copy, and this brings the negotiating of the agreement to a close.

Stage Five Closure

> **What would people like to take away from this today?**
>
> **What has been the learning?**
>
> **What do you think we have achieved here together?**
>
> **Who is taking responsibility for what?**

The closing phase will include reminders of follow up actions and completion of evaluation sheets.

Thank everyone for the choices they made in coming and their efforts in helping to resolve this matter together is important. Appreciation of how far they have come towards repairing the harm will also highlight what they have achieved.

Finally an invitation to refreshments provides an additional bonding and reintegrating experience to follow the challenges of the meeting. People need to have a chance to relax outside the formality of the conference. In our experience this is often where some of the deeper restoration can occur and the rebuilding begin. There's nothing like a shared 'nice cuppa' for getting people closer! This again can be a powerful ritual in terms of mending relationships and getting people re-connected.

CHAPTER 8
Does it Work?

'Everyone learns from their mistakes. If they don't learn the first time, they'll probably learn the second time. It's really up to them'

Vanessa Cuevas, Met Secondary school pupil, Virginia

Stories and Evaluation Research

In this chapter we take note of emerging research and evaluations occurring nationally and internationally and listen to some stories of restorative solutions that have taken place. In considering the impact restorative work has had in schools and communities to date, we will cover and report on:

→ Reductions in exclusions

→ Reduced levels of Bullying

→ Impact on non - school attendance

→ Improved Behaviour across Schools and Communities:

   International Research

   Research in England and Wales

   Scottish Research

→ Impact of Family Involvement and Support

→ Making deeper spiritual and human connections

→ Conclusions on research

So does this way of working actually work? As we write, evaluations of Restorative work in the UK and across the world are taking place. Much of the research is showing significant benefits to participating communities and individuals plus high levels of satisfaction reported from those who have directly engaged in the processes. Time and attention has been provided for victims of harm doing. People are being listened to and agreements maintained. After a rigorous look at all the research on restorative justice worldwide, Strang and Sherman conclude among many other positive conclusions that:

Crime victims who participate in restorative justice do better, on average, than victims who do not, across a wide range of outcomes including post-traumatic stress.

In many tests, offenders who participate in restorative justice commit fewer repeat crimes than offenders who do not. (Strang and Sherman, 2007)

So, are offenders learning and changing? The indications are very optimistic. This is the messy world of relationships. Not all the research variables can be controlled however rigorous we might try to be, but the promise of alternative structures to exclusion processes feels closer when schools adopt a more restorative perspective as can be seen from what follows. Often the narratives are where the true power lies.

With only three exceptions (all from the same school), all school staff interviewed believed that their school had benefited from having restorative justice approaches available to them.

The school has benefited in many ways. It's helping to change the culture, recognising that others have feelings, and saying sorry. Talking things through is not the way that people do things around here; it's not part of their upbringing at home. This is making a big difference. (Head teacher)

Restorative justice was seen as a time-saver, a catalyst to culture change, and a strategy to enable staff to work in more productive ways. It allows children (and parents if involved) to be listened to and have a voice. If practised well, in the right circumstances, it also produces mostly sustainable outcomes. It has allowed me to step away from behaviour management issues. (Head of year)

Youth Justice Board, 2004

One of the first questions any decision maker may have about introducing this way of working in school will be "Does this really work and where is the evidence in terms of changing attitudes, beliefs and ultimately behaviour towards others?"

Few evaluations existed for schools in the UK who pioneered working restoratively under the Restorative Justice in Schools Program funded by the Youth Justice Board for England and Wales. There was some UK research specific to schools carried out in May 2000 but prior to this there was very little, and much of the research on restorative processes tended to be drawn only from related research carried out internationally in New Zealand and elsewhere (Maxwell and Morris, 1993, Jackson, 1998).

The Crime and Disorder Act 1998 provided a statutory context in the UK for commitment at government level to provide a wide ranging and creative new infrastructure and set of interventions within the field of youth justice. For the first time restorative interventions had a statutory status and were introduced as part of sentencing options for the courts. It was the first indication of the government's growing interest in restorative methods and victim's rights. The Youth Justice and Criminal Evidence Act 1999 then also explicitly endorsed restorative principles supported by a research base around the effectiveness of these interventions (Tickell and Akester, 2004). From the late 1990s we can see a range of attempts to explore the implementation of restorative working in Youth Justice situations. Educators were soon keen to be involved too in tackling issues related to behaviour, bullying and non-attendance.

Restorative justice – bringing 'victims, offenders and communities together in response to a particular crime' – is an example of effective, but resource intensive and controversial policy. One example has been the notion that offenders should face up to their actions and make amends to their local community for their crimes by undertaking community service. This has been tried by Crime and Disorder Reduction Partnerships (CDRPs), which have ensured that responsible authorities, such as the police and local councils, interact with other local agencies and organisations to develop and implement strategies to tackle crime. Pilot studies have indicated that reparations, made as a part of a community-based sentence, are effective in motivating offenders to turn away from a life of crime.

(New Local Government Network, June, 2007)

What impact has restorative work had in schools and communities to date?

Humiliated teacher

Paul, a year 8 boy in a UK Comprehensive School annoyed Mr Moore, a Maths teacher by throwing a scrunched up ball of paper at him during a lesson. The ball of paper hit Mr Moore on the head, and although unhurt, he felt angry and humiliated, as the rest of the class took it as a chance to laugh at him.

Initially, Mr Moore wanted Paul to be excluded for a number of days, but was persuaded to take part in a Restorative Conference, facilitated by one of his colleagues. During the Conference, Mr Moore was able to explain to Paul in a calm way how he felt about what had happened in his classroom the day before, and how it had affected his family. (He had gone home that evening in a very bad temper and had had an argument with his wife).

Paul apologised to Mr Moore, promised that he would try to behave better in his lessons, and then volunteered to clean out the maths stockroom, a job, which Mr Moore had been putting off for about 2 years.

Reductions in exclusions

The University of Waikato New Zealand (during 1999-2000) were assigned by the Ministry of Education to pilot and develop a process for using Restorative Justice for conferencing in schools local to the University. This was in response to the sharp rise in the suspension/exclusion of pupils, both at primary and secondary stages. Maori boys, in particular, were identified as being over represented in the exclusion figures.

Five schools with very different characteristics were involved in that pilot project and showed that they implemented the ideas in very different ways. (Drewery, Winslade and McMenamin, 2002)

The participants in the project were satisfied with the outcomes of the pilot, which included significant reduction in exclusions, and following this, the project was expanded to involve 29 schools in the region. Restorative conferencing was acknowledged as a powerful intervention in a school context, and has now widened its net to incorporate and develop a range of restorative practices.

Forest Hill Community School, ... has been using restorative justice for four years, and was one of the first in the country to do so. All the other schools in Lewisham, as well as other agencies - the Youth Offending Team, school police officers - have since been offered training in its strategies. The school faces the usual inner-city challenges such as disaffection, deprivation and a high number of children who don't speak English at home. All its pupils are boys and it is big - 1,400 on the roll. Yet it is oversubscribed, and has an excellent pastoral reputation.

As Mick Levens explains, however, its reputation for strictness used to be achieved partly through high levels of punishment. Permanent exclusions ran at a general rate of six a year. Last year there were four and this year, so far, there have been none. Short-term exclusions are down by nearly three quarters and even relatively minor misbehaviour is drastically reduced - the proportion of children being sent out of lessons to the school's "time out" referral room has almost halved. ... Originating in methods used by the Maoris, the technique is gaining in popularity in Britain. Cherie Blair recently called for its use to bring criminals to an understanding of the impact of their wrongdoing. (The Independent, April 12th 2007)

In the UK restorative justice conferences sit alongside mediation, internal exclusion and managed moves as alternatives to permanent and fixed term exclusions. They hold enormous promise with their formality and own structured processes. This promise has yet to be clearly reflected in national evaluation studies.

It is difficult to ascertain exactly the impact of restorative justice practices on school exclusion, as exclusions are affected by a number of factors. First, schools have developed a number of strategies to reduce their exclusion figures. Second, many of the schools in the study had not made any fixed-term exclusions during the period for which the key data were collected. Third, there were multiple interventions in all schools to improve behaviour and to reduce exclusions, making it impossible to tease out the effect that restorative justice had on reducing exclusions. Finally, school exclusion rates are also subject to changes in school leadership and behaviour policies. Some schools used restorative justice conferences to reintegrate pupils after fixed-term exclusions. Twelve of the programme schools in the study used restorative justice in some way in relation to exclusions, either to prevent them or to reintegrate into school pupils who had been excluded for a fixed term. (Youth Justice Board, 2004)

The 2004 national evaluation whilst revealing a complex picture regarding the number of exclusions did include positive comments about the effectiveness of restorative approaches on reducing school exclusions from the key stakeholder interviews.

It's taken the heat out of some major feuds between pupils and avoided exclusions.
(In-school restorative justice co-ordinator)

We have avoided fixed-term exclusions with all 14 of our conferences.
(Behaviour co-ordinator)

I see it as a civilising approach. It can help to keep the student in school. It leads to inclusion, not exclusion. I'd rather keep them in school. Exclusions are seen as a holiday. Long may it continue. (Head of year)

Youth Justice Board, 2004

In 2006 there was an evaluation of Restorative Group Conferencing in three of Milton Keynes, UK schools. One outcome from this very optimistic study was the finding that the risk of exclusion had been reduced because the cause had been removed with the resolution of the conflict. In the majority of cases where there was a possibility of exclusion the situation improved after the Restorative Group Conference. As one young person puts it:

Because if you don't like them or do stuff or have a go at the teacher and use swear words there is no point just getting excluded just dead on the spot, because you haven't heard both sides of the story so you think you just have a conference and then you hear all the sides of the story don't you? (Milton Keynes Educational Psychology Service, 2006)

Reduced levels of bullying

Restorative justice processes offer us an opportunity to get off the seesaw between punitive and moralistic approaches to addressing school bullying. Advocates of punitive approaches call for responsibility and accountability for behavior. Advocates of the libertarian approaches call for further care and support of the person. A restorative process involves both these components, in that: (1) a message is communicated to the offender that the behaviour is not condoned by a community; (2) the offender is offered respect, support and forgiveness by the community. In other words, efforts are made to separate the act (or behaviour) from the person. (Morrison, 2001)

The first and best-known intervention to reduce bullying among school children was launched by Olweus in Norway and Sweden in the early 1980's inspired by the suicides of several severely victimized children. Norway supported the development and implementation of a comprehensive program to address bullying among children in school. The program involved interventions at multiple levels:

Schoolwide interventions. A survey of bullying problems at each school, increased supervision, schoolwide assemblies, and teacher inservice training to raise the awareness of children and school staff regarding bullying.

Classroom-level interventions. The establishment of classroom rules against bullying, regular class meetings to discuss bullying at school, and meetings with all parents.

Individual-level interventions. Discussions with students identified as bullies and victims.

This predominantly restorative program was found to be highly effective in reducing bullying and other antisocial behavior among students in primary and junior high schools. Within 2 years of implementation, both boys' and girls' self-reports indicated that bullying had decreased by 50%. These changes in behaviour were more pronounced the longer the programme was in effect. Moreover, students reported significant decreases in rates of truancy, vandalism, and theft and indicated that their school's climate was significantly more positive as a result of the programme. Not surprisingly, those schools that had implemented more of the programme's components experienced the most marked changes in behaviour. The core components of the Olweus anti-bullying program have been adapted for use in several other cultures, including Canada, the UK and the United States (Olweus, 1993). The use of restorative justice conferencing in schools has received mixed reviews and the uptake of the practice has been slow in the UK, Australia and other countries (Morrison 2001). The current evidence suggests that what is needed is broader institutional support, in the form of a culture shift that supports the process (Ritchie & O'Connell 2001).

Bullying is a difficult but ever present issue for schools to tackle. Levels of bullying can vary, but everyone is likely to experience bullying at some point in their life. International tragic incidents resulting from bullying continue to make regular media headlines.

A significant group of pupils will be being bullied in every school as we write this book. This issue, whilst much higher profile in recent years is still challenging for must traditional school discipline systems, which typically have very little impact (Sharp and Smith, 1994). Restorative interventions appear to offer something more, and have proven effective in tackling bullying (Cameron and Thoresborne, 2001) especially when the peer group is actively involved (Cowie, 2000).

Bullied by a Gang

Helen was a Year 10 girl in an inner city comprehensive. Small for her age, she had been teased and bullied about her appearance for many years, but the problem reached a new intensity when she was surrounded by a gang of eight girls in the school yard and subjected to ten minutes of constant haranguing and taunting. The incident was seen by teachers who stopped the girls, and after talking to Helen, finally realised the extent of the problem. Various strategies had been tried over the years both with Helen and her tormentors, but nothing had really worked.

Restorative Approaches had just been introduced into the school, and Helen's head of year decided to try to resolve the situation by setting up some meetings run on Restorative lines. However, Helen was unwilling to meet face to face with her eight tormentors, even though she desperately wanted the bullying to stop. Her head of year managed to arrange eight separate meetings where the themes that had been identified in Helen's thoughts and feelings were addressed with each child at the appropriate points. Each one had a different experience and perspective and the responsibility of the facilitator was to ensure that there was a detailed accounting of what happened, the thoughts and feelings of those whose actions caused the harm and how it was experienced by Helen. This proved to add to the effective experience of it with the context being set for each individual and helped them relate their side of the story and the impact of their actions on Helen. To varying degrees, the eight girls were shocked at how Helen felt about what they had thought was a harmless game. Most of them volunteered to "become her friend", while the others said that they would "leave her alone". Helen's last three terms at school were her happiest, and she ended up gaining some creditable GCSE results and enrolling in the local FE college.

In the UK restorative interventions have been directed at bullying with increasingly positive outcomes.

Bullying has decreased in the Lambeth programme schools by 4% and 7%, while it has increased in all the other schools, with the greatest increases occurring in the non-programme schools (5% and 13%).

Verbal threats significantly decreased in the Lambeth schools, with an increase of 13% of pupils reporting that they have not been verbally threatened by another pupil in the past month (p<0.05)

In Somerset, there was an 8% reduction in reported bullying in the programme school, and a 14% increase in thinking that the school was doing a good job in stopping bullying. Meanwhile, in the non-programme school, pupils reported an 11% increase in rumour spreading, and an 11% decrease in thinking that the school was doing a good job in stopping bullying.
(Youth Justice Board, 2004)

The general term, "whole school approach", has been around internationally for some time. Under the "whole school" umbrella restorative anti bullying programs in schools have combined community dialogue among students, teachers and parents on how to prevent bullying with mediation of specific cases (Rigby, 1996). The evaluations of results have been positive (Farrington, 1993; Pitts and Smith, 1995, Rigby, 1996).

In 2006 the Milton Keynes study showed that conferences were effective in the three schools evaluated, in addressing bullying cases as evidenced by questionnaires, reviews and interviews.

Research in North America also demonstrate that restorative conferencing programs have been very successful and the anti bullying programs with a restorative ethos have managed in some cases to halve bullying in schools. (Farrington, 1993).

Peer involvement in restorative interventions such as peer mediation, peer counselling and Circles of Friends are proving to be a rich and effective way of impacting upon school bullying (Cowie, 2000, Newton and Wilson, 2007).

Impact on Non-School Attendance

Restorative approaches in Japanese schools, as evidenced by Masters (1997) in his qualitative research, have been shown to be very successful with radical "whole school" innovations. One case example cited a school principal doing three home visits to a girl and her mother. This pupil had been verbally insulted by the whole class and was refusing to return. The class teacher also guided the class through a process of restorative reparation. The agreed resolution involved a visit by all of the class to the girl's home, where apologies were offered and forgiveness requested. A report was given to the entire school staff following the incident the restorative interventions and the final outcome. The class apologised to the staff group for taking up so much of their time (Cummings, 1980, cited in Masters, 1997).

Lynn Zammit (2001) reported that the introduction of restorative justice into one school in Arizona, USA had the following effect on truancy:

	1998-99	1999-2000	2000-2001
Truancy	16%	5%	-

In the UK the Nottingham Restorative Conferencing Project (2002) evaluated a series of 105 conferences in 8 schools and reported that attendance improved in each where this was an issue. 78% of conferences were judged successful and 16% partially successful when measured against the criteria that 'issues had been resolved'.

Stalking

This story concerns Sandeep (14) and Emma (13) who both attended the same inner city comprehensive school and were in the same teaching group for some subjects.

The school's Education Welfare Officer (EWO) was doing a routine check and noticed that Emma had truanted from two particular lessons on every occasion in the past two weeks. When he talked to Emma he discovered that she was happy to attend all other lessons, but she would not tell him why she was leaving school to miss English and History, except to say that it was "nothing to do with the teachers or the work."

The Education Welfare Officer passed the case on to an experienced senior member of staff, who had a good relationship with Emma and to whom she felt able to talk about what was happening to her. She was missing English and History because of a boy in her class called Sandeep; these were the only two lessons where they were in the same group. Emma explained to the teacher that Sandeep made her feel very uncomfortable. For the past 3 or 4 weeks, he had been staring at her, had followed her around the school yard at breaktimes, and had followed her home on one occasion, sitting on a wall outside her house for a couple of hours until it got dark. The only way she felt she could deal with this was to avoid him, thus missing some lessons.

The teacher realised that Emma wanted to tell Sandeep about how she felt, but had no way of doing so. She suggested a Restorative Conference for the next day, and Emma agreed. Sandeep was also invited and told what the issue was about. He seemed keen to participate.

The teacher facilitated the Conference the next day. Emma told Sandeep that his behaviour made her feel uncomfortable and scared and that she had had to truant to get away from him. Sandeep was horrified to discover the effect his behaviour was having: he had no real explanation for his behaviour, except that somehow he "really liked" Emma. He made a firm agreement to Emma that he would stop harassing her. He kept to his agreement and two weeks later intervened sensibly in the yard when two older boys began to call Emma names.

We don't always know what becomes of cases like Emma and Sandeep's beyond the follow up, if everything is going well. What we do know is that the Restorative Conference repaired Emma and Sandeep's relationship in the short term, and that Emma missed no more lessons. Sandeep not only became aware of the effect his behaviour was having on someone else and didn't repeat it in his final two years at school, he also became sensitive to the effects of other boy's words/actions. As we can see from this example, he was then able to intervene in a restorative way by prompting them to reflect on the effects of what they were saying. Whilst both Sandeep and Emma were invited to come back to the restorative justice coordinator if things were not working out and if there continued to be any ongoing issues, they did not. It was important to keep open the option to talk even after the follow up. The fact that neither came back led all concerned to assume that the longer-term outlook was good and informal checking about how things were with their form tutors evidenced this.

Southend Local Authority in Essex, UK (2002-3) studied the first eight conferences that were run in their Southend Family Group Conference pilot project. It set out to establish the viability of using this process in education and to establish its effectiveness when used with problems of attendance and to see how participants perceived it.

The study, while only with a small group of pupils, demonstrated clearly that in the majority of children attendance did rise significantly, in one case as much as 74%. It was least effective when the young person did not attend the meeting, and was not part of the planning process. The study also showed that even if this is the case attendance still appeared to rise.

Individual school attendance pre and post conference

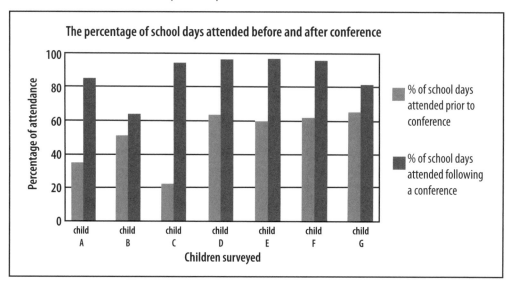

School attendance for pupils in the programme varied from 23 – 69%. The average attendance for pupils in the four pilot schools was 81% compared to 93% nationally. Attendance levels rose to 97.2% for one pupil following a Family Group Conference with an average attendance being recorded at 87.4% immediately following a conference. One pupils' attendance improved only slightly (from 51% to 64%) post conference; this pupil did not attend the conference. Her attendance subsequently rose in the months following the conference to an average of 85%. One pupils' attendance rose from 23% to 91% post conference. Her attendance continues to average at 92% (McGrath, 2003).

Improved Behaviour across Schools and Communities

Research in England and Wales

In New Zealand there are reports that the use of Family Group Conferencing done rigorously alongside community work in the Wellington region had the following effects between 1994-1999:

⟶ Youth Crime reduced by 70%

⟶ Repeat offending within one month of the previous crime, reduced from 36 to 2 per year

In practice, our research on family group conferences showed that:

→ *Victims were willing and able to participate in restorative justice processes*

→ *A significant proportion of victims felt positively toward the process and were satisfied with the outcomes*

→ *Offenders were held accountable*

→ *Reconviction rates were no worse and may be better than for court-based samples*

→ *Factors in restorative justice processes may be linked to a lower probability of reconviction.* (Maxwell and Morris, 1998)

Action research undertaken by researchers from the University of Waikato between 1999 and 2001 (Drewery, Winslade and McMenamin, 2002) with some 34 schools in New Zealand, was very optimistic in outcomes. It gave practical details for others implementing such approaches. Their findings largely echo what is described below in the UK context, especially the involvement of the headteacher and managers, the importance of training at least two people in every school and the impact upon a school culture of such an approach.

A restorative approach to school discipline represents a major change in attitude for many schools, away from the retributive approach to discipline that is so familiar to most of us in the education system. Nevertheless, our interactions with the schools who participated…suggest that there is a strong desire among school hierarchies to embrace a less confrontational approach to school discipline. (Restorative Practices Development Team, New Zealand 2003)

Lynn Zammit (2001) reported that the introduction of restorative justice into one school in Arizona, USA had the following effects:

	1998-99	1999-2000	2000-2001
Referrals for Discipline	3,786	945	625
Physical Assaults and fights	841	28	18

An example of a restorative justice programme for which robust outcome data exist is the Halt Scheme from the Netherlands (Coester, 2002). The Halt Scheme, an extra-judicial response to acts of vandalism committed by young people, offered those arrested the possibility to work or pay as a means of rectifying their offence. Since the early 1980s, when the programme was established, the objective of the Halt Scheme has broadened to address offences other than vandalism, including theft and shoplifting. Research from the programme's pilot stages indicates that the Halt Scheme has had positive results in terms of reducing recidivism. After contact with the Scheme, over 60% of the young people reduced offending behaviour or ceased to commit acts of delinquency, compared to a control group where 25% committed fewer criminal acts, but where none stopped completely.

Research in England and Wales

Thames Valley **Restorative Cautioning and Conferencing** was piloted in Aylesbury, in the UK as an initiative for adults as well as for young people and was inspired by the example of New South Wales. In the latter Australian setting, restorative conferences had been introduced to encourage people to take responsibility for their actions and to improve relationships in that context between police and the community (Tickell and Akester, 2004).

The 2002 evaluation of the Thames Valley scheme showed that the participants were mostly satisfied and valued the opportunity to meet and to express themselves. They thought on the whole that the aims were met and outcomes were satisfactory. Comparative studies of young offenders aged 10-17 indicated that those who went through the restorative process at cautioning stage were only **half as likely** to be re-sanctioned within a year.

Importantly, the evaluation underlined the importance of getting the process right. It named the following examples of bad practice:

→ Poor quality facilitation

→ Under-preparation of parties

→ Coercion of young people or their supporters

→ Lack of clarity of purpose leading to misunderstanding

→ Relationships deteriorating leaving the young person feeling a "bad person".

Police working for the Bourne End Restorative Justice Unit also incorporated restorative conferencing as part of their cautioning process. About 20 cases were dealt with each week and police officers were impressed with how effective and powerful conferences could be (Miers et. al. 2001). Sir Charles Pollard in 2006 reported that:

'The victim is 15 times more likely to get an apology than in the court process, two fifths are less likely to suffer impairment in their daily life and work, and 97 per cent said their conference 'went well'. Of 46 studies, 41 showed fewer reconvictions, 2 showed neutral effects, and only 3 showed some evidence of increased re-offending. It faces threats, including over-professionalizing, lack of resources, and media scare stories; the latter need to be countered by case studies.' (Pollard, 2006)

In 2004 a pilot initiative using restorative justice conferences to tackle exclusions, truancy, bullying and other forms of anti-social behaviour was launched in two schools in the London Borough of Lambeth. The program was extended to Hammersmith and Fulham, and two other London boroughs. Following positive indicators it was extended to some other areas across England and Wales. Nine Youth Offending Teams (YOTS) in total covering 26 schools, 6 of which were Primaries began using restorative practices.

An audit within one of the Hammersmith and Fulham schools provided quantitative and some qualitative feedback of pupils' experiences of the restorative conferences. This was independent of the national evaluation and provided a more accessible and instant evaluation specific to that school. Questionnaires were given to pupils who had participated in the conferences and these were completed voluntarily. 60 returns from children and young people were received and the results of these were presented within an OFSTED inspection in June 2005.

91% of pupils made agreements in the conferences. The percentage of pupils who felt they were able to tell their side of the story was 94% with the remaining 6% answering "not sure" rather than not at all. 97% of pupils felt the conference agreement was 'fair' (Clark and Mahaffey, 2004).

Details were taken from the request for involvement information. This clarified whether the conference itself was instead of exclusion, post exclusion (reintegration) or if the incident itself did not warrant exclusion. Sometimes this was because the issue was connected to a relationship matter that needed to be resolved. This school was particularly interested in whether restorative conferences had any impact on reducing exclusions. 65% of conferences occurred instead of giving fixed term exclusion, with the remaining 35% being 'not applicable' since the incident itself would not have warranted fixed term exclusion.

Some of the comments from the young people themselves in this audit included:

It was a really good way to deal with the problem with the other boy

It's the fairest thing in this school

They could see how I felt

Subsequent to this, one OFSTED inspector actually commented that the restorative process helps in "working towards improving behaviour", and at the same time "not enough people have access to it" (Clark and Mahaffey, 2004).

The restorative practice coordinator for the school actually commented:

If this is what a difference it can make in one school think what a difference it can make in all schools if it is carried out and monitored properly!

From 2001- 2004 a national evaluation was carried out by the Youth Justice Board across the pilot projects of the UK. The full report, '**National Evaluation of the Restorative Justice in Schools Programme**' (2004) can be viewed at:
http://www.yjb.gov.uk/Publications/Scripts/prodView.asp?idProduct=207&eP=

Data was collected for each school at the beginning and at the end of the evaluation. This included contextual data (such as the percentage of pupils receiving free school meals and the school roll) and performance indicator data (such as exclusions, attendance, staff sickness and turnover, and the number of restorative conferences).

All Year 7 and Year 9 pupils in the participating secondary schools completed victimisation questionnaires before the interventions were introduced (4,604 pupils).

The survey was repeated in each of the schools with the same year groups between January and March 2004 in order to find out whether the restorative justice initiatives had made a difference to the levels of victimisation, bullying and degree of safety felt by pupils. Their attitudes were also measured according to a number of key variables such as their perceptions of how well (or how badly) the school was doing at stopping bullying, and whether telling a teacher about being bullied was seen as 'grassing' (tale - telling).

This evaluation showed that the restorative justice interventions including restorative justice conferences organised by school staff together with outside agencies such as YOT staff, police or mediation service staff, were making a positive impact. In some places school staff were trained to implement restorative practices or to develop peer mediation processes. A variety of restorative interventions were implemented during the national programme ranging from restorative enquiry to circle time.

One case in the research involved a student admitting to setting off a fire alarm between lessons. The conference that was held included the local fire safety officer, the young person and his mother, another pupil who had recently set off the alarm prior to this and a school representative. The student's mother felt that the conference was far more likely, to make her son take notice of the seriousness of what he had done compared with just being told off or punished by school.

Girl Gangs

An incident occurred between two girl gangs from different schools when, following a death in one of the girl's family, one girl received a text message saying: "Ha-ha, your brother's died!"

The girls from one gang threatened to attack the girls in the other gang outside their school. One of the girls in the threatened gang asked a member of the school staff to intervene and asked for a conference (she had been party to another incident that had been resolved through a conference).

A conference was organised between some of the girls from the two schools. Five girls from each school attended. The girl who had received the text was not present at this conference. A number of relatively minor issues between the two groups were discussed in the conference, and all agreed to stay away from each other in future.

A further incident occurred between the two gangs when a girl from one gang barged another in a shopping centre, resulting in a further escalation of the threats. It was agreed to hold another conference. This time the girl who had received the text message attended. The facilitators skilfully handled the large group of girls in the conference. During the second conference it emerged that two of the girls had switched their gang allegiance and that one of the girls had a cousin who was being bullied by the girls in the other school. These events were the real source of the dispute. Feelings were aired, and those present agreed that it was good to be able to talk about what had happened and the problems that these incidents were causing all of them. It also emerged that other people in the gangs were stirring things up, and trying to keep the conflicts going.

After much talking, the girls again agreed to pay less attention to those stirring and to keep their distance. This time the agreement between the two gangs held.

Youth Justice Board, 2004

The summary of the National Evaluation of the Restorative Justice in Schools Programme (2004) demonstrated in its outcomes that a total of 92% of conferences resulted in an agreement. The agreements themselves revealed that what the restorative conferences had brought forth were:

→ Apologies

→ Repaired relationships

→ Stopping of behaviour that led to the conference and

→ Maintaining of distance between the parties, through formal reparation.

One of the significant findings was that only 6% of conferences failed to reach a satisfactory agreement. For the remaining 2% of conferences a final agreement had not been reached at the time of reporting but follow-up conferences had been planned to address this.

The value and sustainability of the agreements was demonstrated by the three-month follow up interviews. These indicated an impressive 96% of the agreements had been upheld and only 4% of the agreements had been broken within this time period.

The qualitative interviews revealed that those who participated perceived that the approach gave pupils and parents a voice and that restorative conferencing had a positive impact upon communication between staff, parents and children.

Pupils reported high levels of satisfaction with the process of participating in conferences, with 89% of pupils reporting that they were satisfied with the outcome of the conferences and 93% reporting that they thought that the process was fair and that justice had been done. Having an opportunity to be listened to and being heard was highlighted as the most important part of the process:

"It was a chance to sort things out, to get over what had happened before, and start again for the future"   (Year 6 boy)

"What was best was that she told the truth. I expected her to make up all sorts of lies about me"   (Year 7 girl)

"Bringing everyone together to sort things out is better because you can hear what one another say, instead of being separate. It cuts down on people lying"   (Year 8 boy)

"The teachers treated us the same. We were both allowed to make our points of view, but no one person got more time than the other. It was fair"   (Year 9 girl)
(Youth Justice Board, 2004)

Staff felt more enabled to work in more productive ways and generally the approach was seen as offering new approaches to solving longstanding problems. Survey findings about pupil behaviour showed that there had been a significant improvement in pupil behaviour in the programme schools, while behaviour had declined in the non-programme schools.

Of staff in programme schools, 6% more reported that pupil behaviour had improved since the introduction of restorative approaches (statistically significant p<0.05), while there was a 5% decrease in staff in non-programme schools who reported that pupil behaviour had improved. There was a 9% reduction of staff in programme schools who reported that pupil behaviour had worsened between the two surveys, while there was an increase of 12% of staff at non-programme schools who reported that pupil behaviour had worsened.

"It has been very effective. It has worked with some of the toughest pupils in the school and the agreements have largely been upheld. It has reduced the cycle of retaliations after incidents, and has reduced aggressive behaviour in those that have been involved" (Social inclusion assistant)

"The conferences help young people to separate facts from emotions. It has helped perpetrators to be more aware of the effects of their actions and to take responsibility, particularly where they thought things were just a joke, and they had not realised the impact their behaviour was having on their victims. It has also helped to increase the confidence of victims" (Deputy head, secondary school)

"I know from the children that I have worked with that have been through restorative justice, that it has made a big impact on them. Some became the best of friends – others simply agreed to say hello and stay apart" (Head of year)
(Youth Justice Board, 2004)

In this evaluation although the numbers were small, it seemed that staff who had specialist roles in dealing with behaviour (supportive curriculum staff and special needs staff) also tended to have a negative view of restorative approaches. They reported that restorative approaches were "nothing new", or spoke about the dangers of allowing non-specialists to interfere with a specialist role. Some of these specialist staff also had a particular concern about the possible stigmatising effect of working with the police in a conference.

One conclusion of the work was that restorative justice is not a panacea for all situations. It is argued that it needs to be targeted at the right people, at the right time, by people with the right skills and within a whole-school approach for it to be maximally effective.

"Restorative justice is a clear process in terms of a way to manage a meeting with a definitive outcome which all the parties are clear about. Students and parents have welcomed the clear agreements which result at the end of the conference" (Head teacher, secondary school)

"Staff running conferences must be skilled – they must be secure in what they're doing. They must feel safe" (Police officer)

"We deal with bullies every day – it needs to be dealt with on the spot. To leave it a week till someone from the Yot comes in is way too long" (Head of year)
(Youth Justice Board, 2004)

Not surprisingly, an integral part of implementing restorative practices in schools appeared to be head teachers' commitment. It was actually considered to be one of the most important factors in getting restorative practices properly embedded in school practice. One of the single most important factors in the introduction of restorative approaches into schools is acceptance on the part of the head teacher. The influence of the head teacher on the school culture and ethos is paramount. If restorative approaches are introduced without their full commitment in both vision and practice, it was concluded, they will not be fully effective. This point was strongly reinforced by all the key stakeholders interviewed other than head teachers.

Restorative
Solutions

But it is clear that restorative justice needs to be led from the top by someone with a vision about how restorative practices can add value to the school.
(Youth Justice Board, 2004)

Clear information was seen as being important. This included details of what restorative justice is, how it is to be implemented and by whom. Schools needed to commit time and resources for this work to be effective. These included in-service training for staff on restorative approaches and the lack of this was seen as the single biggest barrier to implementation.

Senior managers in schools were asked what levels of resourcing would be necessary to sustain the project. The variations in costings needed to sustain the project varied widely (from £6,000 to £20,000 per year), to fund a proportion of a staff member's time to run conferences (learning mentors, counsellors, etc.). Others thought that only training costs needed to be provided (approximately £1,500 per annum).
(Youth Justice Board, 2004)

In the 2006 Milton Keynes study, students considered that conferencing had a positive effect on relationships and conflicts in schools and recommended the approach to be introduced in other schools.

Scottish Research

The Scottish Executive (government) provided funding for a 30-month pilot project in three Scottish councils (recently extended by a further two years) beginning in 2004. The overall aim for the pilot projects was to learn more about restorative practices in school settings and to look at whether there could be a distinctive Scottish approach, that is, an approach that both complemented and offered something additional to Scottish practice. The three pilot councils developed their restorative projects in different ways, although they worked with the Scottish Executive to develop a broadly common underpinning philosophy. Eighteen schools were identified as pilot evaluation schools; these included ten high schools, seven primary schools and one special school, in urban, suburban and rural areas and in areas of severe economic poverty as well as areas of relative economic wealth. They had varied histories in terms of existing approaches that could be described as restorative and had very varied expectations of the project. The universities of Edinburgh and Glasgow conducted a two-year formative evaluation of the work (Lloyd, 2006).

The 18 schools progressed at different speeds, primary schools in general finding it easier to develop whole-school approaches. In every school, as expected, staff were at different stages of knowledge and commitment; in some most were strongly involved and there was a sense of critical mass, of changing culture and ethos. However, the evaluation was able to identify real strengths and achievements across all councils and schools. Students and staff, particularly in primary schools, identified measurable improvements in school climate and student behavior. They described restorative language in use by staff and students. In one school, visitors commented on the air of calmness. Students felt valued by staff and were able to identify restorative elements in their teachers' actions. Primary schools had not made much use of disciplinary exclusions, but where they had this was eliminated or significantly reduced, and there was clear evidence of reduction in referrals to managers for discipline and in some cases a reduction of the need for external behavior support.

"Now it's OK to be seen (by other staff), to be talking things through—not necessary to be seen to punish" (a teacher).

The high schools were more diverse in their achievements. Several had recently undergone critical external evaluation and changes in head teachers that slowed the process of change. However, there was clear evidence of changing cultures and practice. In some there was still a significant challenge from a minority of resistant staff; in one school there were strong feelings by a vocal minority that this kind of approach represented an undermining of proper discipline. In others, however, there was clear evidence of a school "turning around," with significant reduction in use of punishments and of expulsion. In most high schools, staff had substituted restorative processes for more traditional punishments such as "lines," although in some, former punishment processes still remained alongside them. (Lloyd, 2006)

This may not be the only "answer" to issues of relationships and discipline in schools, and some of the elements may not be entirely new. However, our evaluation indicates that it has a great deal to offer. (Lloyd, 2006)

Impact on Family Involvement and Support

It is significant that restorative justice approaches, as opposed to punitive and stigmatising responses, have demonstrably reduced delinquency when parents have applied the principles and practice in raising their children (Braithwaite, 1989; Sampson and Laub, 1993). Participation in restorative approaches have also been reported to result in more positive contact with schools:

> *Everyone had a chance to speak. I definitely felt listened to by the school, and also my son.*

> *It has helped us to communicate better with our children at home too, trying to listen more instead of blaming.*

> *It's good when a phone call comes through now to tell you something good.*
> (Paddy O'Connor, Principal, Letterkenny, Vocational School, Ireland, 2004)

Braithwaite's claim (1989) is that because so many families so often slip into 'stigmatisation and brutalisation' of their difficult members, we need restorative justice institutionalised in a wider context that can engage and restore such families. Schools within this context play a vital role within an ethos of care and integration as part of the educational ideal. Families can learn the principles of restorative interventions with support and encouragement.

In the UK research (Youth Justice Board, 2004) less than a fifth (19%) of conferences involved parents as parties to the conference. Parents were routinely involved in conferences in just five schools, although a further 10 schools involved parents in more serious incidents. Parents were not involved in 11 schools. What is equally striking from this research is that when parents were involved even more progress was made and relationships strengthened.

"We had one parent attend who had a really bad opinion of the school. After the conference, they went away with a completely different view of the school. We have a much more constructive relationship now"   (Head teacher)

"We involve parents whenever we can, mainly when the incident is serious. It takes time to make all the calls, and this is really important. We let them know that everyone will have a chance to have their say and to be listened to. We stress that your child is not a bad child and that you are not a bad parent. We need you to come into the school because so-and-so is happening and we want to work together to solve it. When they come in we are not in the head's office and no one is laying down the law to them. They see me as a person who's there to resolve the issue. It's not threatening for them because we make sure that it is not so"
(School counsellor/Restorative justice facilitator)

"It makes a huge difference having the parents in the conference. It enables them to have a voice, and it shows that the school is trying to work with them, rather than against them"
(YOT restorative justice co-ordinator/facilitator)
(Youth Justice Board, 2004)

Involving parents may be challenging for busy school staff but the payoffs are likely to be rich if this and other emerging research is anything to go by. Parents can learn to be more restorative and can strengthen agreements made between individual pupils. Parents are more likely to get a sense of partnership or at least a feeling that they are working with the school rather than against each other.

Playground Aggression

Steven in Year 3 and Danny in Year 6 had an argument in the playground about a football. Danny lashed out at Steven and hurt him, by slapping him around the face. The 2 boys had previously got on really well, but Steven's mum was very angry and refused to countenance any action apart from some kind of punishment or retribution. She wasn't even sure what it would be: she just wanted something doing, and was very resistant to the idea of any Restorative approach. However, the deputy head of the school persisted and eventually and grudgingly Steven's mum agreed to a short Restorative Conference taking place. His bigger brother supported Steven and Danny had a friend from his class to support him.

After about 20 minutes, the problem was resolved. Danny agreed to keep away from Steven, but also agreed to say "hello" and would smile whenever they met. Both boys said that they "felt better" after the conference. Steven's mum pronounced herself "astounded" by the difference the conference made and became a firm advocate amongst other parents for the Restorative Approach.

Making deeper spiritual and human connections

International commentators on restorative approaches to conflicts and those directly involved in reconciliation activities on a large scale in parts of the world such as Northern Ireland and Southern Africa emphasise the importance of **forgiveness, active listening and resolution**.

Each process of healing through restorative justice is an opportunity to create deeper community bonds while building social capital and creating more heart-based solutions to local problems. The capacity of restorative justice to address these emotional and relational needs—and to engage the citizenry in doing so—is the key to achieving and sustaining a healthy civil society. An international restorative/peace approach to international conflicts has been proven to drastically reduce deaths by war and other forms of violence. (Pip Cornwall, 2007)

International peacemakers speak up for the deeper most meaningful connections between people that restoration invites. Desmond Tutu speaks of the South African concept of **ubuntu**, an ancient Bantu word - the essence of being human. Ubuntu reflects that we:

*… **live in a delicate network of interdependence. … That a person is a person through other people. … I am human because I belong. I participate, I share.** (Tutu, 1999)*

The desire for community connection with other people stands in paradox with the desire for individuality and human expressions of freedom. Restorative approaches nurture the former instinct. Three of the regularly reported outcomes of working restoratively in the UK are summarised by Hopkins (2004) as:

→ The reduction of fear

→ Enhancement of harmonious relationships

→ Improvement in self esteem

The enhancement of harmonious relationships is at the heart of human connection and peaceful community building.

Long Term Dispute

Two Year 9 girls, Rebecca and Emma were brought together after two and a half years of difficulties and problems. Many "friends" on both sides had become embroiled in the disputes, and the school was aware that as the girls got older two gangs were on the point of forming. After one nasty incident, a teacher brought the two girls together and ran a meeting on Restorative lines. After 40 minutes the girls agreed to make up and asked for all their friends to be brought in one by one so that they could be told "its all over".

Rebecca said, "That half hour sorted out more problems than the previous two years had." Emma said that they had never been brought together to sort out their issues, and had realised within 10 minutes of being together that no one wanted the situation that had developed. The girls just didn't know how to solve the problem.

Subsequent checks and support by the school showed that Rebecca and Emma are still OK together, and a potentially unpleasant situation between two gangs had been averted.

The indigenous communities of North America, Canada and New Zealand have provided inspiration and cultural resources throughout the world. These cultures bring a depth and "spirituality" to their community processes which have enriched restorative justice (Braithwaite, J., 2003). This has not been without its own challenges for implementation of this work in the UK and elsewhere, as Drewery, for example, outlines:

…the value underpinnings of euro-western psychology and indeed euro-western education are in fact contrary to many fundamental values of Maori culture such as whanaungatanga (interconnectedness) and manaakitanga (care and hospitality). (Drewery et. al, 2003)

Notice the similarity between ubuntu and whanaungatanga, Bantu and Maori both reaching for the connectedness of humans with each other. This is being echoed in the findings of Western physicists as they note how we are all physically part of one another at a sub atomic level.

Working more restoratively takes us deeper, helping us to listen to and understand what lies underneath behaviour and between people. Inevitably this involves us in a newer, deeper story, perhaps as described so eloquently by Margaret Wheatley (2005):

It is the story of how we feel when we see people helping each other, when we feel creative, when we know we are making a difference, when life feels purposeful.

In conclusion…

The research is building and paints a predominantly positive picture, even if restorative work is not the ultimate panacea or 'silver bullet' for all the challenges of our society. Restorative work holds great promise for tackling the challenges of conflicted relationships and hard to manage behaviour in our schools and communities.

Whilst this data is always hard to interpret the number of exclusions do appear to have been impacted upon positively. Bullying has been reduced in most studies that have examined this. Some support for improved levels of attendance is beginning to emerge. Improved levels of behaviour in schools and communities seem well evidenced by agreements being kept, by reductions in crime and positive reports especially from people who have been harmed.

Hardly surprising but there is clearly documented resistance from a range of stakeholders to these changes in practice. Families have been positive about their involvement in restorative processes and there is some evidence for processes being used in the home as well as by school based and other practitioners. What also appears to be emerging is a shift in thinking away from 'blame and punishment' as the default mode when practitioners are confronted by challenging and rule breaking behaviour. Deeper spiritual and human connectedness appear well nurtured by a more restorative approach to relationships. Ultimately it appears that we can create a new story for how we respond when harm occurs in our schools, families and communities.

Restorative justice as a new paradigm has much promise and its power to change lives has sometimes been underestimated. But it is no silver bullet. Sometimes it proves no more effective (or, in some cases, even less effective) than traditional criminal justice procedures. Its effectiveness is also dependent on the circumstances surrounding the offence and the offender. Nevertheless, the evidence to date strongly supports the continued and concerted use of restorative justice, with careful attention to the accumulation of further evidence about the conditions under which it proves to be most effective. (Strang and Sherman, 2007)

Resolved with a Kiss

A Reception teacher is attempting to work restoratively with two reception aged pupils. Darren had pushed Jameel over onto the yard, causing his head to be grazed.

When asked the question 'how can you make it right?' Darren apologised.

The teacher then said 'What else can you do?'

With this Darren leant over and kissed Jameel on the forehead!

We would love to hear of your own stories and research to add to this exciting and rapidly developing field of activity.

'If we care about kids more than we
care about schools, then we must
change schools' Anon

Policy, Practice and Guiding Ideas

In this chapter we reflect upon:

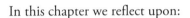

→ Drawing together the strands

→ Our vision of a restorative school

→ Guiding Ideas:

→ The Behavioural Perspective

→ The Humanistic Perspective

→ Cognitive theory

→ Systemic Theory

→ Social constructionism: a framework for restorative thinking and action

→ The metaphor of The Fifth Province

→ The Circle of Courage

Drawing together the strands

So it's clear, you need a Relationships Policy in your school. This will support practice
throughout the school whenever harm or offence is caused.

Creating this will not be easy. You can expect resistance, the reappearance or persistence
of old habits and a resurgence of the enemies or gargoyles of change: control, fear and
complacency. All the champions of change detailed in Chapter 3 will need to be in place.
Remember the medicine wheel cycle: leadership – vision – community – management.

Belinda Hopkins, in her 2004 book – Just Schools – makes links between school
improvement activity in general and developments in Restorative Practice.

*…ultimately a restorative justice project will be much more effective if it is part of a whole
school approach, in which everyone in the school community is using restorative skills on a
daily basis.*

Once established, your school's Relationship Policy will expect all practitioners from midday supervisor to head teacher to think and act restoratively as their first instinct whenever harm has occurred. Repairing harm, mending relationships and truly listening to individuals who have been harmed will run through the school team like the letters through a stick of seaside rock.

Processes such as Circle Time and curriculum areas such as PSHE (Personal, Social and Health Education), SEAL (Social and Emotional Aspects of Learning) and Citizenship will be firmly built into the school day rather than 'add ons' to academic achievement. Friendship and Relationships are now major concerns rather than distractions or afterthoughts.

Mediation schemes involving peer support and pupil mediators will be alive at all break times and will involve pupils from across the school. Anti bullying strategies using peer counselling and peace making processes will be activating the wider pupil body to sustain a school ethos of restoration.

When more serious incidents occur and something formal must be done, short conferences will be held by trained staff across the school.

When major incidents occur the key senior members of staff will have the facilitation skills available to them to be able to run full restorative conferences involving pupils, staff, parents and wider community members as necessary.

Every effort will be made to fit creative and participatory responses to pupils with emotional needs. The same responsiveness will be present for others who seriously challenge those involved in their care and education and there will be little evidence of more rigid approaches to rewards and sanctions.

A restorative school is emerging, peace has truly broken out!

T here's nothing so practical as a good theory (Einstein)

Guiding Ideas

Restorative practices are coherent with many theoretical frameworks. The Scottish approach acknowledges the theoretical framework underpinning other approaches to supporting children in schools. These include humanistic, person-centered psychology, cognitive-behavioral approaches, the "social model" and sociological perspectives on social and educational processes that recognize conflicting purposes of schooling. (Likewise the developing theoretical model on restorative justice in Scotland draws less on criminological perspectives on harm/shame and more on person-centered and cognitive perspectives. See www.restorativejusticescotland.org.uk.) Thus, restorative approaches recognize the human wish to feel safe, to belong, to be respected and to understand and have positive relationships with others. They acknowledge the potential of social and experiential learning approaches that enable students (and staff) to understand and learn to manage their own behavior. They recognize the fundamental importance of both effective support and clear control and boundaries in schools. (Lloyd, 2005)

A number of writers have pointed to what appears to be a paradigm shift in the way we are viewing and dealing with behaviour and relationships in both the Criminal Justice system and in formal school discipline structures (Hopkins, 2004). We appear to be moving from a predominantly **retributive** system for delivering school discipline to one that is much **more restorative**. Some authors have even suggested that the two positions are not mutually exclusive (Zehr, 2002). We believe that this paradigm shift in UK schools is essential if the number of exclusions and segregated placements for pupils who present challenging behaviour is to decline.

Restorative Justice is a river...started as a tiny trickle in the 1980s, an effort by a handful of people dreaming of doing justice differently. It originated in practice and in experimentation rather than in abstractions...Thousands of people from around the globe bring their experience and expertise to the river. The river like all rivers exists because it is being fed by numerous tributaries flowing in from around the world. (Zehr, 2002)

Where and how exactly will the river flow? What will the river bring with it? What will the river need to erode? What obstacles will the water flow around or over? What kind of a paradigm shift will UK schools be part of?

Within this "flow" it will be useful to have a set of guiding ideas, theories and metaphors to draw upon and help us to keep orientated. Some of these concepts and ideas will be familiar and some schools already draw upon these theories and ideas to help solve problems.

In the following section we describe a range of theoretical models that have been used to understand behaviour change and we relate these models to restorative practice.

The Behavioural Perspective

The thinking behind the behavioural perspective is that all behaviour occurs because it is reinforced. If unacceptable behaviours have been learned then they can be unlearned and replaced by more desirable ones. Many programmes of behaviour modification follow the simple plan of rewarding good behaviour and ignoring bad. A 'modelling' process is also used which is based on the idea that children can learn good behaviour by imitating behaviours to be learned and those to be avoided. In general teachers tend to like behaviourist approaches as they are optimistic, based on the belief that behaviour can change and because they are quite easy to use in the classroom.

The focus of this perspective is on a pupil's overt, observable and measurable behaviour. The perspective takes no account of cognitive factors (thinking and problem solving processes), underlying emotions or unconscious processes. It views an individual's behaviour as the result of their past and present learning experiences and the focus is on the current and observable environmental events that are assumed to be triggering and maintaining the observed behaviour. The emphasis within this perspective is on changing pupil's behaviour through external methods (rewards and sanctions) rather than through the person's own resources.

It also pays little attention to context and relationship when trying to understand issues of behaviour. From this perspective the same sanctions or rewards should work equally well whichever member of staff is applying them.

The appeal of the behavioural approach is that it is simple to understand and has a considerable degree of overlap with what might be called a 'common sense' approach to behavioural management - reward what you want to see more of and apply sanctions to the behaviours you want to see less of. This is pretty much the default setting of most schools' behaviour policies.

As a restorative practitioner, you will need to become very good at making clear the limitations of this perspective whilst also holding onto some of what it has to offer. The emphasis within the behavioural approach on precise descriptions of what the problem behaviour is and encouragement to make more objective measurement of its frequency can often be helpful in clarifying ways forward even if these do not involve reward and sanctions. Thus a behavioural formulation of a behaviour issue will likely have the following structure:

→ A precise, clear and specific description of the problem behaviours

→ An hypothesis as to what events are triggering and maintaining the behaviours

→ An idea as to how these problems could be managed via increasing appropriate and decreasing or extinguishing inappropriate behaviours

Behavioural approaches have been most typically applied at the level of the individual pupil, at group or class level (see **http://www.adprima.com/assertive.htm** for more on the use of the behavioural perspective at a whole class and at a school policy level)

The behavioural approach has had some strong critics and foremost among them within the educational context is American writer Alfie Kohn - author of Punished by Rewards (1993) his paper of the same name (available through the following link - http://www.alfiekohn.org/teaching/pbracwak.htm) is well worth a read and will be helpful to you in developing your 'restorative solutions script' around the issue of using rewards and sanctions in educational settings.

The Behavioural perspective loosely informs many of the behaviour management and sanction systems in our primary and secondary schools at the time of writing this book. However this perspective has left many practitioners and families frustrated in the face of complex emotional needs and re-occurrences of challenging behaviour. The theory is of limited use to our understanding of restorative working but we include it here because of its prevalence in our usual responses to children's behaviour and for its helpful emphasis on clearly describing behaviour.

The Cognitive Perspective

The cognitive perspective (sometimes known as the 'Cognitive-Behavioural' approach) was developed in response to some of the perceived limitations of the behavioural perspective discussed above. Within the cognitive perspective more attention is paid to the thinking, reasoning and problem solving processes that underlie behaviour.

The basic assumptions of this perspective are as follows:

→ Cognitive processes are associated with behaviours

→ Cognitive processes can bring about changes in behaviour

→ Cognitive processes can be assessed, change and evaluated

The Cognitive perspective is an approach to help people experiencing a wide range of mental health difficulties. The basis of the approach is that what people think affects how they feel emotionally and also alters what they do. Restorative working does draw upon this perspective as young people are directly encouraged to reflect upon their past and future choices and actions through such key scripted questions as: **'What were you thinking about at the time?'**

During times of mental distress the way a person sees and judges themselves and the things that happen to them alters. Things tend to become more extreme and unhelpful. This can worsen how the person feels and causes them to act in ways that keep their distress going.

A range of types of intervention fall within the cognitive perspective alongside more restorative interventions including; anger management training, (useful summary at: http://www.indiana.edu/~safeschl/AngerManagement.pdf) stress inoculation training, self instruction training, problem solving skills training, social skills training and so on. Additionally, much of the approach adopted in the widely known work by Bill Rogers (2004) falls within the cognitive perspective. What these approaches have in common is methodologies that aim to teach students to think differently about a situation before they act, a key aim of restorative working.

Amongst the most helpful insights from the cognitive approach and one that can be of most use to restorative practitioners is the belief that teachers can gain insight into what they may regard as unpredictable behaviour if they understand that people construct meaning from their world from their experiences. People perceive different experiences differently and teachers cannot assume that the meaning behind what they say is the same meaning placed on it by students. Communication can be misconstrued and bring about different responses to behaviour. The cognitive perspective is likely to be of most value to you as a restorative practitioner in carrying out interventions at an individual pupil or whole class level.

The Humanistic Perspective

Another perspective that is relevant to Restorative working is the humanistic perspective. This directs our attention most clearly to the role of emotions and feelings as the triggers underlying challenging behaviour. This perspective also helps us appreciate that all learning has an emotional component and is premised on pupils and the adults who teach them feeling emotionally and physically safe, feeling that they belong and are valued and having successful learning experiences that allow them to grow in feelings of confidence and competence. It is the perspective that is most explicit about the fact that teachers have feelings too and that effective leadership in restorative work creates structures for these feelings to be acknowledged, explored and used as a means of further understanding the pupils involved and generating strategies to deal with the issues arising.

Within the humanistic perspective, difficulties with behaviour are largely viewed as resulting from low self esteem and/or difficulties with feelings (in either the pupil or the teacher or both) and therefore this perspective anticipates that changes/improvements in behaviour will be driven by subjective changes in how the person is perceiving themselves and managing their feelings.

Over the last 5 years there has been increasing attention in the literature to how the insights of the humanistic perspective can be used to impact at a whole school level through activities that enable young people and their teachers to foster an emotionally literate environment.

Two websites that give a grounded account of these processes in action are: **www.creative-corner.co.uk/schools/tuckswood** (a First School) and **www.westborough.kirklees.sch.uk** (a High School).

There is much within the Humanistic Perspective that provides food for thought for aspiring restorative practitioners. The humanistic perspective can help us locate opportunities for change at the level of the individual pupil (through helping them identify and mange their emotions more successfully) at the whole class level (through using emotional literacy activities e.g. circle time to develop group cohesion and supportiveness) and at the whole school level by attending to the emotional needs of the staff team and through the creation/nurturing of leadership styles and whole school policies that reflect the core insights of the humanistic perspective. Finally, it is the perspective that is most likely to help you in clarifying with others the values base of a relationship/behaviour policy or intervention. Rooted as it is in a deep belief about the importance of education, it is the perspective within which respect for others is core.

The relevance of this way of thinking for restorative processes needs hardly spelling out and makes sense of so many underpinning values and processes already described throughout the book.

Websites / Resources related to this perspective:

> **www.antidote.org.uk** – resources relating to an emotional literacy audit

> **www.nelig.com** – the national emotional literacy interest group – disseminates good practice

The Systemic Perspective

Among the perspectives considered in this Chapter, the systemic perspective is the one that pays most attention to the **context** in which the harm is occurring and is thus highly relevant to Restorative practice. It also has important insights to give us on the nature of cause and effect within human relationships. It is also the perspective that is best placed to do justice to the inherent complexity and inter-relatedness of the ways we respond to episodes where harm has occurred.

The guiding set of ideas that underpins the systemic approach is 'systems theory'. There is not space here to do justice to complexities of systems theory but it does provide us with some useful metaphors that can be used by restorative practitioners to encourage deeper thinking around the issues that confront them.

Systems theory would see a school as being rather like a weather system that has many connections to other weather systems. Changes in one system will have effects on other systems in ways that are not always obvious. Thus changes in family systems can impact on school systems and vice versa. This means that the chain of cause and effect is not always obvious and in fact the systemic perspective encourages us to view the causation patterns of challenging behaviour and attendance as essentially circular rather than simply linear. The systemic perspective encourages us to engage in 'big picture thinking' and to pay attention to how changes in the bigger patterns of behaviour can be seen as linked to changes in other related systems. It can help us make links between changes in curriculum organisation and delivery and behaviour, links between an increase in unemployment rates within a school's catchment and changing patterns of behaviour.

The systemic view considers the reciprocity of relationships. For instance, if something happens to one member of a family, or other group it will affect the rest of the family or group, whose response, in turn, will affect the behavior of that individual. This means that behaviour cannot be studied in isolation without taking into account the situation in which it occurs.

In the field of counselling or psychotherapy, the systemic approach is mainly associated with family therapy. The basic assumption underpinning all versions of family therapy is that the distress or difficult behaviour of individual family members is best understood as a manifestation of something going wrong at a systemic level: for example through ineffective communication between family members or some distortion of the structure of the family group. The emphasis is on what goes on between people rather than what takes place **inside** them.

A systemic approach places an emphasis on the role of context of actions and pays close attention to the interactive processes within relationships and the different levels of meanings for each participant. Each participant is seen as being part of a peer group, family, school and community.

"There's always the risk that when the going gets tough, restorative work is an easy target in any school. … You've got a kind of default setting among teachers saying 'well that's all very well but we're not punitive enough, we're not scary enough. The kids aren't frightened of us'" (a staff member) (Lloyd, 2005)

In the process of perceiving, interpreting and understanding new information, this theoretical perspective explores the different contexts in which we are raised. This will include type of family, our culture, education, religion, race, ability in relation to learning and physical factors, and finally the social and political climate in which we live. Each of these different contexts bring values, beliefs and morals within which we operate, govern ourselves and determine what is right and wrong. These factors all have implications to how people get heard and how we hear others.

Drewey, Winslade and McMenamin (2002) suggest that sometimes it is actually not possible to "hear" what someone else is saying because "the parties do not have the same understandings or concepts that are being used by the person they are trying to talk with".

Valuing different viewpoints is central to systemic practice. Each individual constructs his or her own "truth". Within this framework there can therefore be "multiple truths" in any one episode. This can be helpful especially when we see the kinds of "stale mate" positions children get into about what gets said or understood and misinterpreted. Many "truths" can get tangled, misunderstood, and confused. Sometimes the restorative conference disentangles a web of misunderstandings or misinterpretations attached to a conflict in order to restore connections between those involved. The goal of someone working systemically is therefore to facilitate change at a systemic level: for example by rewriting implicit rules, shifting the balance between different parts of the system or improving the effectiveness of how communication/feedback is transmitted.

Importantly, the systemic perspective also gives us fresh ways of looking at the complex triangular relationships that can grow up in the interactions between the child, family and the school and fresh ways of intervening if negative cycles of interaction have become embedded.

In common sense terms the systemic perspective reminds us that human behaviour can readily become subject to 'vicious' circles of interaction and influence and that, if we accept this, it follows that we may be able to intervene in ways that set up benign or 'virtuous' circles of influence.

The systemic perspective is also powerful in helping us move beyond locating the causes of challenging behaviour within any single part of the system. This approach considers problems to be the outcome of cycles of interactions between parts of the system, all of which contribute to the maintenance of the problem situation. If we accept this analysis, it follows that we have an increased range of options for intervention because we know that changes in one part of the overall system will inevitably lead to reciprocal changes in the other elements.

The systemic perspective is likely to give us the best handle on influencing how the family-school context maintains issues of behaviour. By focusing on interactions between the family and the school systems, restorative practitioners are likely to uncover scenarios where school staff regard parents as hostile to the school because when confronted with the problem behaviour of their child they respond negatively, accusing the staff of victimisation. Because of this staff feel their initial perceptions were correct. The child feels vindicated by their parents' accusations against teachers and the problem behaviour continues. A familiar enough vicious circle in many education settings. The practitioner, working from the systemic perspective will analyse this set of interactions without attributing blame or searching for the one definitive cause of the behaviour or locating the cause within a particular individual. The analysis will attempt to understand how each of the participants perceives the behaviour of all of the others, respecting the fact that there are different and equally valid interpretations of the same situation. The practitioner will then use the analysis to attempt to 'reframe' the behaviour in a positive and plausible way. Thus the parents' 'hostile' behaviour is reframed as 'fiercely protective' of their child and a reflection of their fear that the child is becoming more and more solitary and isolated. The practitioner leads a problem solving session with key staff to consider this reframing and to look at ways that the school system can address parents' fears with the outcome that it is decided to introduce the parents to the idea of setting up a 'circle of friends' or to carry out a restorative conference with key stakeholders.

There is no doubt that the systemic perspective is a complex one and it can be hard to encourage staff to recognise the wider systems issues that are at play in challenging behaviour. Despite this, it is a very powerful perspective in as much as it allows practitioners to factor out attributions of blame in the overall description of what is happening and thereby removes a major barrier to facilitating change. http://www.users.globalnet.co.uk/~ebdstudy/strategy/ecosys.htm is a useful source of further information on the systemic approach with suggestions for further reading.

Social Constructionism: A Framework for Restorative Thinking and Action

Problems are stories people have agreed to tell themselves

Social construction theory (Gergen, 1985, Burr 2003) holds that what we know evolves not within the individual brain or nervous system but within the densely languaged give and take between people.

…the process of understanding is not automatically driven by the forces of nature, but is the result of an active cooperative enterprise of persons, in relationship (Gergen, 1985)

Social Constructionist theory is useful in understanding conflicts and their restoration because of its emphasis on different socially constructed 'realities' and its recognition that we all see the world differently.

Methods of enquiry requiring participation and exploration of the meaning within situations rather than objective observations are useful in helping us understand how Restorative practices might have their effect.

A social constructionist framework has been clearly identified by those researching the field of conflict resolution as a useful way to think about interpersonal conflicts and what helps in practice (Beth Fisher- Yoshida 2003).

Wendy Drewery and colleagues (2002, 2005) within this social constructionist framework, use techniques from narrative and positioning theories which assert that some ways of talking to each other are "more respectful" and "more healthy" than others.
A key concept within narrative theory is the use of **externalising language**.

'Externalising' is a concept that was first introduced to the field of family therapy in the early 1980s. There are many ways of understanding externalising, but perhaps it is best summed up in the phrase, 'the person is not the problem, the problem is the problem' (White, 1995).

By the time children and young people, their families or teachers recognize the need for restoration, they have often got to a point where they believe there is something wrong with them, that they or something about them is problematic. The problem has become 'internalised'. It is very common for problems to be understood as 'internal' to people, as if they represent something about the nature, or 'inner-self' of the person concerned.

Externalising practices are an alternative to internalising practices. Externalising locates problems, not within individuals, but as products of culture, context and history. Problems are understood to have been socially constructed and created over time.

The aim of externalising practices is therefore to enable people to realise that they and the problem are **not** the same thing. There are many ways in which this is approached. One way is through asking questions in which we change the adjectives that people use to describe themselves, ('I am an **angry** person') into nouns, ('How long has this **anger** been affecting you?' or 'What does **anger** tell you about yourself?'). Another practice of externalising involves asking questions in a way that invites people to personify problems. For instance, when working with a young child who wants to stop getting into so much trouble, an externalising question might be: 'how does that Mr Mischief manage to trick you?' or 'when is Mr Mischief most likely to visit?'. Through these sorts of questions, some space is created between the person and the problem, and this enables the person to begin to revise their relationship with the problem.

Externalising language, allows for the problem to be the problem and not the person. All problems can be externalised: bullying, blame, fear, anger, and so on depending upon the issue in question. The process of externalising enables everyone to look at the effects of the problem on everyone in a more neutral way. This allows those involved keeping the problem in perspective and considering who might be enlisted in removing or keeping the problem away. Externalising can be used throughout full conferences or in brief restorative interventions.

As people step back and separate from the problem and then consider its history and negative effects, they can find themselves standing in a different territory than the one they have become used to. This different territory is often a place free from practices such as self-blame and judgment.
As the problem is de-centred, what becomes centred in the conversation are people's knowledges of life and skills of living that are relevant to addressing the problem. These become the focus of exploration. Also, once the problem is understood as separate from the identity of the person concerned, it becomes more possible to identify family and friends who can form a team to support and sustain their efforts in reducing the problem's influence. With shame reduced, and problems no longer internalised, collective action becomes more possible (Maggie Carey & Shona Russell, 2007).

The language and actions within the restorative process can become vital to living the process and creating new meaning. This is why there is the need for restorative practitioners and facilitators to model respectful language such as that shown in the box below.

I am not saying you are a good or bad person, but let us look at what has happened and who has been affected by those words and actions. Then we can explore together what needs to happen to put things right and to find a way forward with this.

Celtic Mythology - The "Fifth Province" as a Helpful Metaphor

In our experience of working in schools and youth settings it can be helpful to have a range of different metaphors available to you to describe to participants what a restorative conference is all about. The '**Fifth Province**' is one such metaphor and it has its origins in Celtic mythology.

Geographically, Ireland had four provinces. Irish mythological narrative tells us that Ireland has a Fifth Province, which is not a geographical place, but rather, an invitational place of the mind where questions may be explored utilising confidence, creativity, imagination, an open mind, and different ways of 'seeing'.

The Fifth Province has been described as being at the centre of Ireland and a place where pagan priests and druids used to resolve conflicts through dialogue. Some philosophers have argued that this came "to represent a disposition of empathy and tolerance", Helderman and Kearney (1982).

> The 'fifth province'... is a place within each one of us, that place that is open to the other, that swinging door which allows us to venture out and others to venture in.

McCarthy (1994) and McCarthy and Byrne (1998) directly related the fifth province to their therapeutic practice "where in all emotions, judgements, and descriptions can find acceptance". It was used as a powerful and creative way to create a space where multiple perspectives could be held. – "A neutral ground where things can detach themselves from all partisan and prejudiced connection" (Hederman and Kearney 1982)

For facilitators of a restorative conference, the metaphor of the "fifth province" acts as a useful reminder to take a listening position and not to judge or interpret. It enables the holding together of contradictory stories and sometimes-unequal positions. In this way there is a greater likelihood of bringing forth responsibility and accountability in participants, especially in the person who has harmed or hurt another.

We have used the fifth province as a valuable metaphor when working restoratively. It has proved useful both in a conference situation where holding opposing points of view, and in larger conflicts with groups of young people who by their own description are "at war" with each other. In classroom restorative circles it has been effective in enabling the exploration and holding of different viewpoints. It has provided a very concrete and visual space in working with primary school children. All sorts of creative art and story projects have emerged that build on the ideas and principles that emerge from the "fifth province".

The Circle of Courage Perspective

Finally we offer the Circle of Courage as an excellent way of understanding behaviour, relationships and their emotional underpinnings. This guiding set of ideas is inclusive and respectful and sits very well with restorative practice. This perspective may also prove to be the most useful for understanding the power and effectiveness of restorative interventions.

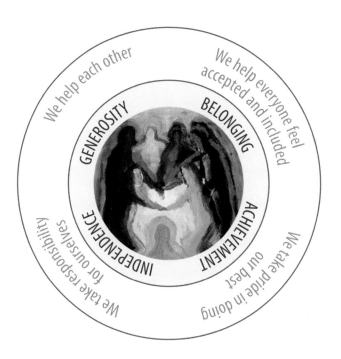

The "Circle of Courage" developed by Larry Brendtro, Martin Brokenleg, and Steven Van Bockern (1990) is just one of hundreds of models for explaining why people do what they do and how we should treat others and educate students (especially those with emotional and behavioural problems). It is based on a Native American/American Indian orientation toward life (specifically how the Sioux Nation might view life), but overlaps with the models of many other cultural groups. It matches up nicely with the views of Western psychology (as promoted by Rudolph Dreikers 1964, among others),
The Circle of Courage model can be used to identify the source of behavioural problems, and guide our restorative and other interventions. The model is presented visually as a wheel with four spokes or supports that keep the wheel "true" and strong.
The most important component, upon which the other three are based, is a well developed sense of "Belonging". Humans have a need to feel valued, important and protected by others...to feel comfortable and welcomed within a group: family, friends, colleagues, etc. Of course the family and close community are the most important influences on the original development of this area of self-esteem. Those who have a weak sense of belonging due to a disrupted or non-supportive upbringing are often able to rebuild or strengthen that area by developing close allegiances, friendships, and relationships later in their lives with positive people and groups. However, those who do not repair that broken area of self-concept may show one or more of many problems in relating to others. They may join into or identify with negative groups that promote crime or religious hatred or some other distorted views. This connection with negative influences is done in an attempt to feel important and be accepted within a social structure. They may become non-responsive or resistant to the efforts of good people and groups (including counsellors and teachers) because they do not feel worthy of inclusion,

or for fear of being rejected by positive people at some point in the future. In essence, they scare off those with whom they most want to be connected.

If one has an impaired, distorted, or absent sense of belonging, it will probably affect one or more of the other areas. For example, those who have a strong sense of "Generosity" (because those in the groups to which they belonged when they were young shared time, work, play, resources, and knowledge) are empathetic toward others and want to help others. They give of themselves or their possessions in some way. They truly have the "joy of giving", receiving pleasure from helping others in need. Folks who have a distorted or absent sense of generosity will be "stingy", lack concern for the welfare of others, be callous in their interactions with others, and "take" rather than "give".

Those who are strong in the quadrant of "Mastery" feel competent in their abilities, seek more skills and knowledge, and are willing to fail or look unskilled when they try new things. Those with an impaired sense of mastery have a low self concept, fear failure, may refuse to try a task for fear of failure, give up easily, are dependent on others, and/or may devalue and ridicule schooling or the efforts of others.

Persons with a strong sense of "Independence" feel in control of themselves, their behaviour, and their lives. They have a well-developed sense of autonomy, and accept responsibility for themselves and their actions. On the other hand, those who have a lessened or absent sense of independence are likely to engage in "scatter-brained" behaviour, be easily swayed by others, and blame circumstances/others for their actions.

BELONGING is strengthened by experiences of trust, co-operation, attachment, friendliness, acceptance, being included, receiving affection

ACHIEVEMENT is strengthened by experiences of problem solving, being motivated, success in what you set out to do, persisting despite difficulties, creating something, and facing up to a challenge

INDEPENDENCE is strengthened by experiences of making real choices for yourself, self control, being assertive, being confident, and showing self discipline, experiences of leadership

GENEROSITY is strengthened by experiences of being loyal, showing care and concern to others, being empathic and supportive to others, sharing what you have, listening to others troubles, being altruistic and making a contribution to the group/community you live/work in.

As a restorative practitioner the Circle of Courage perspective is likely to be of value to you in your attempts to guide thinking at a whole school level. It maps on well to the outcomes framework of the Children Act 2004 and particularly to the theme of 'Making a Positive Contribution'. However the Circle of Courage perspective can also be of value in informing thinking at both group and at an individual child level as it can direct thinking towards interventions that many other perspectives would be unlikely to generate. This is particularly true of the insights derived from considering the pupil's experiences (or lack of them) within the 'Generosity' quadrant. Restorative working may well provide opportunities for offenders to give back or contribute in the process of making things right.

In fact a successful Restorative Conference should provide the harmed person and the person who has harmed with positive experiences in all the four quadrants of the Circle of Courage.

The process should strengthen their sense of belonging, sense of achievement as a situation is resolved, independence as real choices are made and generosity as giving and being empathic to another are at the heart of this way of working. Let us see how far this way of viewing behaviour and relationships can guide our interventions and solutions?

Websites with further information:

www.augie.edu/dept/nast/Projects/doc6.htm

www.coe.wayne.edu:16080/wholeschooling/
WS/WSPressThe%20Future%20of%20Education.pdf

'Education is not the filling of a pail but the lighting of a fire' W.B. Yeats

This chapter simply goes through a range of questions that are frequently asked about working restoratively. It is by no means an exhaustive set of questions and it would be good to hear from you about other areas of curiosity and interest within this emerging field. We have offered just one of many possible responses and we hope you can develop and add to them. Some questions are reflective of the ongoing debate, which anyone practicing restoratively, directly or indirectly, is part of.

Isn't this just a soft option?

No. Many "offenders" report that the process is a much tougher experience than the traditional punishment or sanction. Many pupils will actually feel benefits from fixed term exclusions where they are sent home for a few days to languish in front of TV or Play Station only to return to the 'respect' of peers. This can be an institutional home goal and it is all too common. Facing up to your victim, having to recount thinking and feeling and possibly encounter a real sense of shame is not easy or comfortable and is likely to lead to real learning and a greater sense of responsibility. It also gives time and attention to the "victim" to express themselves and seek out what they need to help them move on.

How do you get parents on board with this approach?

It is essential to be proactive with parents and carers in the wider local community not just the parents of involved parties in a dispute or incident. Some school leadership teams write to all parents to explain their new approach to relationships and behaviour issues, others invite groups of parents in to school and carry out a professional presentation with discussion opportunities. By being proactive it should be possible to avoid having to react to parents' complaints about an approach that they may label as too liberal, wishy-washy or too soft. Most parents want to know that 'something is being done' when their child is hurt. Restorative approaches should become the dominant way that 'something is done' and can become part of a recognisable culture that parents come to understand. The additional advantage with the restorative work is that parents can be directly involved in the process of making things right.

What if the victim will not attend a conference?

Pupils can be interviewed separately with exactly the same questions and do not actually have to face the other person if they just cannot bear to, or do not feel safe. Video footage, closed circuit TV, web cam can be used or simply, transcripts of interviews can be shared.

Can you punish behaviour as well as restore relationships?

In an ideal world the restorative process would be sufficient.

"A child should experience the consequence of his misbehaviour, but not punishment. The problem with punishment is that it doesn't work, it is a distraction. Instead of the child feeling sorry for what he has done and thinking about how he can make amends, he becomes pre-occupied with revenge fantasies. In other words, by punishing a child, we actually deprive him of the very important process of facing his own misbehaviour. Punishment encourages selfishness". (RJ Handbook, Nottingham 2007)

'Making it right' can be fully accepted as sufficient without anything more overtly punitive being needed. However at this point in our history some school staff and families could still feel the need to additionally engage in punitive sanctioning with a young person. This may be symbolic, showing 'something was done' or reflect a continued hankering for retribution; an eye for an eye. Often it is thought to show the school and parent community that everything possible is being done to stop any reoffending.

Restoration and retribution may not be complete opposites. Ensuring there are consequences for actions lies at the heart of both approaches. The promise of restorative interventions is that they provide a more constructive alternative to exclusion, segregation and incarceration, which are not the only or the best consequences for wrongdoing. Ideally schools will embrace restorative approaches from the most senior levels and create whole school change (Hopkins, 2004). In some situations, change will be slow, may be bottom up, case-by-case, or influenced by the work of outside support agencies. In these settings consequences will be dealt out punitively alongside restorative interventions occurring at least for a time. What might this look like?

In some cases, where a managed move is being considered as an alternative to permanent exclusion, a conference could take place before the move to another school.

Restorative approaches can also be used in a complementary way alongside both fixed term and permanent exclusion. Where immediate fixed term exclusion cannot be avoided, a conference can be set up to precede the child's return to school. The conference should assist their reintegration into school. Where an immediate permanent exclusion cannot be avoided, a conference can assist the child's move to another school and may bring closure to the incident.

I've been teaching 30 years and why should I change my approach to discipline now?

This question was raised by a teacher at a launch conference in the Highlands of Scotland. Sitting right next to him was the Secondary Headteacher of a very large Scottish Academy, who was quick to reply:

'So have I ...but its not working, every year we are excluding a group of pupils, largely socially disadvantaged, poor kids, and they end up knocking around the local estate engaging in crime and behaviour that is just disruptive to our community. We need another, fresh way of approaching things.'

The wisdom was in the room! We do need a fresh and radical way of dealing with wrong doing that focuses on restoring relationships not on sanctioning individual offenders.

How much time is Restorative Working going to take?

Restorative interventions and solutions are time intensive when done properly. It includes the preparation of each party (the larger the number the longer the preparation time) and the conference can take up to an hour (or an hour and a half for a full conference). Both the longer term and immediate benefits however far outweigh the time taken when one considers that ongoing sanctions and punishments have not worked. Young people, who have learned restorative skills from participating in conferences, can be hugely resourceful to many others if invited and supported in imparting their new abilities in helping to sort things out between their peers.

Can Restorative Interventions be used with primary and secondary school age children?

There is no real age limit to this way of working and it has been very successful even in nursery school where children as young as 3 are learning about fairness. Restorative approaches involve empathic listening, restorative discussion, circle time and peer mediation and the sooner children become familiar with and practice these the more reflective they can become of their own actions.

Is Restorative Working just Mediation?

We define mediation as the process to use when there is no clear responsibility from either party for what took place. The process may of course still have a restorative effect. To participate in a fully restorative encounter such as a conference a wrongdoer must admit to some level of responsibility.

Is this just yet another new fashion fad?

No. The roots of restorative justice are probably as old as human history. Native peoples of New Zealand and North America have long approached justice in restorative ways. More recent approaches developed in the 1970s stemmed from the Mennonites applying their faith and peace perspectives to the harsh criminal justice world in Ontario and Indiana. The UK police force learned from fellow colleagues in New Zealand and Australia and initiated developments here.

How can a teacher respond restoratively if a fight breaks out between two pupils when they have a class to manage?

Teachers are often teaching a class of 30+ pupils. First and foremost an incident has to be managed taking into account the safety of all. It may be that both pupils need to be separated and moved from the class and given supervised space to calm down. If they can manage to stay in class, there may be a need to wait until the lesson is finished with a "truce" arrangement. They can then be sent to a member of staff trained in restorative conferencing to do an assessment with a view to running a pupil-pupil conference at the soonest possible time.

How can I contain a conflict whilst I do the preparation for a Restorative Conference?

One idea is to think about calling a 'truce' between the parties in conflict. The first truce we ever used was in response to a large group conflict and it proved to be a stunning device. Group and inter group conflicts inevitably require a number of short conferences and necessitate longer preparation time. We have found that both teachers and pupils have had confidence in a truce and this makes it an effective and powerful tool. Children feel equipped and really understand that it is an 'in between' agreement for peace, while things are being negotiated and getting resolved. One important aspect of this is that it retains the dignity of all sides and no one "loses face". Surprisingly, we have found that a truce actually has some street and playground "cred" being recognised as meaningful and real within the peer group. Young people have actually helped others within their group to keep to their "truce".

What about the complex problem of cyber bullying via mobile phones or computers?

The problem with exchanges that occur via mobile phones or "chat" networks such as MSN and Facebook is that the person causing the harm is not always readily identifiable and this can add to the torment. We recommend group forums such as restorative work in circles (see earlier chapters) within a whole year group to help to bring things to the foreground and to create a sense of group responsibility. We have found that making the issues explicit whilst respecting the confidentiality of the person on the receiving end of the bullying can have an impact. The "grapevine usually reveals who has done it"; in which case we would proceed as with any other restorative conference and involve both parties' parents or carers.

Will it work with cyber bullying?

Yes it can. Here is an example.

A teenage girl in an all girls secondary school at the beginning of year 8 started to receive "hate" email, via a messaging site, from another girl of the same age who believed that she had taken her best friend from her. A bombardment of messages over a period of a couple of weeks was sent taunting this pupil about her weight, looks and family. Deprecating language included calling the girl a "waste of space", "a dog" and "puss face" until the sender became disinterested. Although she stopped sending these types of messages, because of the nature of the site and public accessibility for those who chose to "log on" other girls (totally unconnected to the initial message sending) began to add to it and took over the sending of equally nasty messages seeing it as "a bit of fun".

The pupil on the receiving end of this described being "worried" at first but said that she had tried to block it from her mind. After a few days she described it as really starting to affect her. As the process continued she described even feeling "dirty" as well as being embarrassed and thinking that everyone in the school was looking at her. She started to wonder what awful thing she had done to offend someone and was feeling guilty. One of the hardest things for her was that there was no face to it. She could not work out if it was one or a multiple of people because every message she received had been anonymous (although she described different styles and words used so she guessed it was more than one). She imagined a large group of girls ganging up on her and feared she might come to physical harm eventually in some 'horrible way'.

Over the weeks her attendance dropped and she began missing school altogether. This was actually making her ill and depressed. Her parents had become seriously concerned when she eventually told them about the messages and they immediately took it up with the Head of Year, a senior teacher at the school. One of the main problems for the teacher who tried to address the issue, was that she found it impossible to trace who had been sending the messages and could not understand why the girl had kept going into this website. The Head of Year had attempted to investigate the matter but there persisted in her words "a veil of silence" from all girls in the year. She described feeling "powerless" to do anything more.

The parents experienced this as a lack of action on the school's part and they found themselves increasingly taking an oppositional position to the school in their desperation and frustration. Just as they were about to remove their daughter from the school the staff looked towards a restorative strategy from an independent restorative practitioner they knew. A series of meetings (including: a home visit to the family, meeting with parents and head of year, with the girl on her own) took place with the purpose of negotiating a restorative strategy that fitted for everyone, most of all the girl who had been on the receiving end.

Useful discussions led to restorative actions and initially a series of circles were put in place initially exploring within the frame of rights and responsibilities of internet and mobile phone use. Once there was space created to reflect on this within the safe structure of restorative circles that were run across the whole year group and was theme based, some very rich discussion ensued. This included a conversation about the potential for serious harm and hurt this sort of communication could create without people being aware necessarily of the impact and how out of control and unsafe that could become. All pupils who took part in the circles were fully engaged and able to reflect from different positions. In the process of doing this they were actually learning what it meant to take responsibility for their actions within this context in a general sense. The unexpected outcome (which highlights for us the magic of taking a restorative stance) was when the girls realised the degree of humiliation that could be experienced receiving such negative messages even when the intention might be prankish. This was the "aha moment". Three girls subsequently approached a teacher to admit that they had been part of sending messages of this kind to the girl who had absented herself because of this.

The girl who instigated the messaging also subsequently admitted to it after much peer pressure. This girl's parents were extremely angry with her and were fixed on punishment. They agreed to have a restorative conference (full) however, with the other girl, her parents and the head of year. The girl's parents who had already put in place sanctions such as grounding their daughter and an internet ban, wanted to punish her further but were persuaded against it by seeing the powerful effects the restorative process itself had on their daughter. There were very emotional scenes between the two girls, and the learning was immense. This was revealed in the reflections that were made about how initial actions and choice to send messages of this kind can take on a life of their own and subsequently snowball out of control with others becoming involved. The degree of suffering on this occasion that it led to was poignantly felt by all as a "lived" experience of the girl.

In addition to the individual contracts made between the girls, the question of how children stay safe on the Internet especially in relation to Internet and mobile phone use became a focal point. Both girls were keen to take this forward in a project that they both wanted to work on equally. This was described as having an empowering effect on the girl who had received the messages in the belief that she could do something that could benefit other pupils. It also led to parents, teachers and other pupils working together to share knowledge and expertise to create a leaflet for the school community. Outside of the conference the girl had a different bombardment. This time of welcome back cards, pleasant pictures and warm wishes from the other girls who had been part of this.

I've heard you are not supposed to ask students 'why' they have done what they did when you are working restoratively. Why?

We would advise that the "why" question is avoided at all costs, if it is your intention to work restoratively. Nothing is easier than using the question, 'Why?' when dealing with an incident involving one or more pupils. We have taken the question for granted as it is used so frequently around schools. But it is a word that is often interpreted by the receiver as a precursor to blame or as a word to speed things up as the person who has asked the question is assumed to have made up their mind about the incident. 'Why?' can so easily be experienced as judgemental and confrontational and we therefore discourage the use of this question.

Within a restorative conference, we are looking to use questions that lead to new understandings and to create a space where harm is being repaired. "Why?" becomes redundant. Instead, much care needs to be taken in the choice of alternative questions to use and our intentions in asking them.

But it will never work with......

In fact, this particular thought process comes up regularly as teachers and others try to fit the theory of Restorative Approaches to their work with young people. While this can be a useful exercise, it can turn into a negative experience, as when someone says: "I just can't see how this will work with Emma", or even more bluntly; "This will never work with Emma". An obvious answer is that, of course, we can never be sure what will work and what won't work with a particular individual until we have tried. It is worth making the point that while Restorative work is a very powerful tool and has been shown to work very successfully, it is not the only "silver bullet" of behaviour and relationship management.

Is this for you?
Far-reaching implications of restorative practices in schools

When a school makes a commitment to restorative practices, it is by implication embracing a very different approach to relationships between staff and students, and sometimes amongst staff, from that which may have prevailed until that time. This is because what we are drawing attention to in teaching restorative practices are the ways in which both staff and students show respect for one another, or not. At the University of Waikato we believe the outcomes of a restorative process should include restoring the *mana* of the young person who has offended, of those who have been offended against, and of anyone else whose care for the young person has also been offended against. *Mana* is a Maori word that signals not only respect and personal dignity, it also refers to the agency of the young person. Arguably, an outcome of education for young people is about becoming a sovereign person, an individual with opinions and ideas, who can contribute to society in personally unique ways. That is, education is about citizenship. This is both an individual contribution, and one that must of necessity acknowledge and develop community relationships. Likewise, a restorative process is both transformative of conflicted relationships, and profoundly educational.

Battles for the ethos of the school frequently ensue during the introduction of restorative practices: the primary objection by those opposed to it - often the disciplinarians - can be that it is "nothing more than a slap on the wrist with a wet bus ticket". This response misunderstands the practices as simply disciplinary - and as a weak form of punishment. They are much more than that. In doing this work I have found it strange that it was often the classroom teachers who resisted participation in conferences - even when it may have been their own interactions that had brought the student to this point. Yet when they did come to a conference, teachers almost always found out something about the "problem" child that they did not know before which changed their view completely, and several teachers were so overcome with what they heard that they cried. In such instances we saw relationships between teacher and student transformed before our eyes, such is the power of restorative conferencing.

Conferencing can also transform the relationships between school and home. We saw a school learn, for example, that a young man, brought to conference because of frequent lateness and fighting in the playground, was actually taking responsibility for his younger siblings, and all were being cared for by their grandfather, who was working to keep the family going, against great odds. A useful response to such a situation is surely not to blame such a man, but rather, to find ways to support him. Through a conferencing process, which by its nature brings together a community of care around a young person, the school can learn about the effects of its rules on students' families, and also on relationships between students. By including peers in the conference, it is possible to get a very different perspective on both the problem, and what to do about it. For instance, regular fighting in the playground might be shown up as the effect of bullying, when this had previously been hidden, and called something else.

Used as a disciplinary practice, restorative conferencing becomes another tool of containment, maintaining the boundaries of what is right and what is not. But when the process also defines who is excluded and who is not, in a sense it is a mechanism for policing the boundaries of the school as a community. This is what schools are doing when they suspend or exclude students: they are policing set boundaries, defining who is a member of *their* community. And this process is not what I define as restoration. So we should be very sure about what we are trying to achieve, in becoming a restorative school.

Are we, just possibly, wanting to discipline our students, and **make** them behave, but *in a nice way* – and without examining our own current practices? Embracing restorative practices involves, at least, listening and responding to others whose perspectives may be very different from our own. Are we open to the possibility that profound change may be necessary in how we do things round here, once we really listen to others whose position we have not previously understood?

A restorative school is not primarily about how we police boundaries, but rather, it is about *how we draw* boundaries, and, within that, it is about how we handle difference. It is about inclusion, not exclusion - about community, and how to build it. It is simply not possible to embrace a restorative philosophy while retaining an authoritarian, top down disciplinary system. A restorative philosophy is primarily about how we offer respect towards, and how we provide for the inclusion of, people whose world view is very different from our own, or with whom we may strongly disagree. By contrast, authoritarian discipline is about handing over self-governance to a non participatory, non negotiable hierarchy of power.

Historically, political responses to students' resistance to schooling practices have included placing counsellors and social workers in schools, suggesting that student resistance has been seen as a personal or a social problem related to the individual student, but not as an educational or social one. However, the whole-scale introduction of restorative principles by schools would problematise these individualising positions. The embrace of restorative practices would be nothing short of revolutionary, because it would recognise that responsibility for dealing with problem behaviour is communal and shared. Restorative principles support the foregrounding of relationships of care and community, and they encourage the development of trust and ongoing support. The concept of restoration not only challenges the boundaries between the pastoral care and disciplinary functions of the school: it calls us as a society both to revise our expectations of what schooling is for, and to reconsider the ways we view young people.

But the matter is even more far-reaching than this. Restorative practices can and must also address the issue of increasing social diversity. Restorative practices are about relationship: but not just any kind of relationship. Our attention to restoration also draws attention to how respect can be both offered and taken up. This is especially difficult when those we are in relationship with are very different from ourselves: they may not even share the same basic values. And this kind of respect, across difference, is very hard to achieve.

When those with whom we are trying to relate are like us, it is sometimes difficult to notice how important our common understandings are to how our relationship can go on. When there is little basis of common understanding, it is easier for one side of a partnership to dominate the relationship. One way that this can happen is by the stronger partner determining the terms of the relationship. This happens in schools all the time: the underlying message runs something like "You can come to our school, but you need to embrace our values!"

The terms on which we are each prepared to respect others are at stake in approaching the idea of a restorative school. One way to approach the difficulties that arise in a heterogeneous society would be to screen people who apply for a permit and require that they sign up to certain common values. But is this what we want? No doubt some do, and a commitment to restorative practice is not for them. Most of us however do not want to tell others, or be told by others, what they or we should value. I believe that our relationships with others, especially but not only those who are very different from ourselves, cannot be only what we say they should be (Sampson 1993). If we are interested in a restorative school, each of us needs to be prepared to find that our dearest social values may not be supported by others. It may even be the case that we are initially unable to hear others, because of the dominance of our own ways of thinking. We need to be prepared to try to hear the meanings of the other, to learn about new possibilities, possibly even to change ourselves. This does not mean anything goes or that we should not hold values. But it does mean that we need to remain open to the need to inquire naively about the values of others, and to negotiate when things do not go well.

And maybe there is a bottom line: I notice that empathy is a key ingredient in any successful restorative conference. When the parties learn about the weaknesses and humanness of those who have previously been offenders, opponents or competitors, there is often a kind of catharsis. People can forgive a lot, when they understand how something came to happen. On the other hand, it is easier to befriend or empathise with someone who is like you: harder when they are not. The process of restorative conferencing embraced in this book are deliberately crafted to produce respectful understanding across difference. They do not eliminate the need for discipline and punishment, and they do address wrong-doing, but they do it with an assumption that understanding is possible, just like a family would do, because ultimately we are all on the same side, and we live in the same place.

In many ways, schools are already communities of care, but there is a need for a reexamination of the notion of care that predominates. A community of care is not necessarily one where we have a "natural" or even a learned empathy for others: a true community of care comes into its own when respect is maintained and there is disagreement and strangeness (Young 1990). Such a community understands that meanings are negotiated, and that this can take both time and patience. It understands too the importance of having in place processes for the working through of such disagreements. Where schools care for their students as if they are part of the communal family - including the miscreants, the misfits, and the resisters (of which every family has some) - they are already well on the way.

Schools have a unique and powerful place in our civic life. My vision for schools is also my vision of a restorative society, and schools could have a central role in reaching for this objective. Most of today's schools are already complex communities, reflecting the make up of society, and they are in a powerful position to influence the way forward. This lofty objective will not be achieved by "behaviour management", suspensions and exclusions (though no doubt these must also go on). A primary objective of schooling could be to develop understanding of how to achieve legitimate goals within relationships of mediation in complex communities (Young, 1990). Unravelling what that means in practice will take a while. We can start with small steps, such as the work in this book.

Wendy Drewery
School of Education
University of Waikato
Hamilton
New Zealand

This section contains the full references to sources discussed within the main body of the book and also points you in the direction of a wider range of written and other resources relating to the vision and practice of inclusion and in particular to work with circles of friends or support.

The Internet is a huge source of information and news about inclusive practice; visit our website at www.inclusive-solutions.com for links to a wide range of relevant websites.

References

Clive Anderson show: 5th April 2005 BBC Radio 4

Anderson, H.A & Goolishian, G. Puliam, L. Winderman (1986) *The Galveston Family Institute: Some Personal and Historical Perspectives*. In Efron, D.E (ed), *Journeys. Expansion of the Strategic –Systemic Therapies*, Brunner/Mazel, New York, pp.97-122

Bateson, G. (1972) *Steps to an Ecology of Mind* , London: Ballentine Books.

Bliss, T. and Tetley, J. (1993) *Circle Time,* Lucky Duck Publishing. Bristol.

Blood, P. (2000) *Personal Communication.*

Burr, V. (1995) *An Introduction to Social Constructionism*, Routledge.

Braithwaite, J. (1989) *Crime Shame and Reintegration*, Cambridge: Cambridge University Press.

Braithwaite, J. *Restorative Justice: Assessing Optimistic and Pessimistic Accounts, Crime and Justice*: A review of Research , Vol 25 (ed)

Braithwaite, J. (2003) *Does Restorative Justice Work?* In: Johnson, G (Ed) A Restorative Justice Reader.

Brendtro, L., Brokenleg, M., & Van Bockern, S. (1990) *Reclaiming youth at risk: Our hope f or the future,* Bloomington, IN: National Educational Services

Canter, L. and Canter, M. (1993) *Assertive Discipline: step by step guidelines for effective classroom management,* Published by Behaviour Management Ltd, Bristol.

Cameron, L. & Thorsborne, M. (2001) *Restorative justice and school discipline: Mutually exclusive?,* in J. Braithwaite & H. Strang (eds.), *Restorative Justice and Civil Society,* Cambridge University Press, Cambridge, pp. 180–94. 76.

Clark, J. & Mahaffey, H. (2004) *Restorative Justice in Schools Project* Hammersmith and Fulham Research.

Coester, M., Gossner, U., Rossner, D., Bannenberg, B., and Fasholz, S. (2002) *Kriminologische Analyse empirisch untersuchter Präventionsmodelle aus aller Welt: 61 Studien im Überblick*, in Düsseldorfer Gutachten: Empirisch gesicherte Erkenntnisse über kriminalpräventive Wirkungen, City of Düsseldorf

Cowie, H & Wallace, P. (2000) *Peer Support in Action,* Sage Publications.

Cronen, V. E. & Pearce, W.B. (1989/1990) *The meaning of "meaning" in the CMM analysis of communication: A comparison of two traditions.* Research

Cummings, W.I.(1980) *Education and Equality in Japan*, Princeton: University Press.

De Shazer, S. (1985) *Keys to Solution in Brief Therapy*, New York: Norton.

DfES (2006) Strategy Document: *Citizenship education inquiry 2006.* Citizenship Education: current state of play and recommendations The Citizenship Foundation's written submission to the Education Select Committee Tony Breslin, Don Rowe and Andy Thornton, March 2006

DfES (2006) Head Teacher Standard 6 - *Strengthening Community*, Head teacher Standards.

Dreikurs, R. & Soltz, V. (1964) *Children The Challenge*, Meredith Press, NY

Drewery W, Winslade J, McMenamin D. (2003) *Restorative practices for schools: A Resource,* Human Development and Counselling Monograph Series #1. Hamilton, N.Z.: School of Education, University of Waikato. ISBN 0-9583318-5-5

Drewery, W. (2005) *Why we should watch what we say: Position calls, everyday speech and the production of relational subjectivity,* Theory and Psychology, 15(3): 305-324.

Drewery, W. (2004) *Conferencing in schools: Punishment, Restorative Justice, and the productive importance of the process of conversation,* Journal of Community and Applied Social Psychology, 14, 1-13.

Drewery, W., Winslade, J., & McMenamin, D. (2002) *Restorative practices for schools: Unpublished Report on Northland Project,* Hamilton, New Zealand: University of Waikato.

Faber, A. and Mazlish, E. (2001) *How to Talk So Kids Will Listen and Listen So Kids Will Talk*

Falvey, M.A., Forest, M., Pearpoint, J. and Rosenberg, R. (1994) *All My Life's a Circle-Using the tools: Circles, Maps and Path,* Inclusion Press. Toronto.

Farrington, D.P. (1993) *Understanding and Preventing Bullying*, in Tonry, M. (ed). Crime and Justice: Annual Review of Research. Vol. 17 (Chicago: University of Chicago Press).

Fisher .Yoshida, B. (2003) *Self-awareness and the co-construction of conflict,* Human Systems, The Journal of Systemic Consultation and Management. Vol 14 issues 1-4.

Fox, L., G. Dunlap, M.L. Hemmeter, G.E. Joseph, & P.S. Strain. (2003) *The teaching pyramid: A model for supporting social competence and preventing challenging behavior in young children*. Young Children 58 (4):48–52.

Gelsthorpe T. and West-Burnham J. (eds) (2002) *Educational Leadership and the Community,* London: Pearson Education.

Graef, R. (2000) *Why Restorative Justice? Repairing the harm caused by crime,* Calouste Gulbenkian Foundation, London.

Hammersmith and Fulham Restorative Justice Policy document 2001

Hammersmith and Fulham Restorative Justice in Schools Project Research (2003/2004)

Handy, J. (2005) *Regarding Forgiveness,* in Restorative Justice: Transforming Society, Lockhart, A. and Zammit, L. Inclusion Press

Hanko, G. (1999) *Increasing Competence through Collaborative Problem Solving,* David Fulton Publishers, London.

Helderman , M.P. and Kearney, R. (1982) *The Crane Bag: Book of Irish Studies Dublin,* Blackwater Press

Highfield Junior School, Plymouth (1997) *Changing our School: Promoting Positive Behaviour,* Published by Highfield Junior School and the Institute of Education, University of London. Available from Highfield School, Torridge Way, Efford, Plymouth, Devon PL3 6JQ

Hopkins, B. (2004) *Just Schools. A Whole School Approach to Restorative Justice,* Jessica Kingsley Publishers Ltd. England.

Human Rights Act (1998). HMSO

Jackson, M. (1988) *Maori and the Criminal Justice System Part II,* Wellington; Department of Justice.

Justice (2004) *Restorative Justice.*

Katz, L.G., & D.E. McClellan. (1997) *Fostering children's social competence: The teacher's role,* Washington, DC: NAEYC.

King, Martin Luther (1963) *Strength to love,* Fontana

Kohn, Alfie. (1993, 1999) *Punished By Rewards: The Trouble with Gold Stars, Incentive Plans, A's, Praise, and Other Bribes,* Haughton Mifflin

Kohn, Alfie. (1995) Punished by Rewards? A Conversation with Alfie Kohn http://www.alfiekohn.org/teaching/pdf/Punished%20by%20Rewards.pdf

Kretzman, J and McKnight,J. *Building Communities form the Inside out,* ACTA publications, 1993, pp 210-223

Lajeunesse, T. (1993) *Community Holistic Circle Healing*: Hollow Water First Nation (Solicitor General Canada, Ministry Secretariat).

Lam, J.A. (1989) *The Impact of Conflict Resolution Programs on Schools: A Review and Synthesis of the Evidence*, Amherst, MA: National Association for Medication in Education.

Lewisham Action on Mediation Project (2006) *Restoring The Balance*

Littky (2002) *The Big Picture: Education Is Everyone's Business,* Association for Supervision & Curriculum Development

Lloyd, G., Kane, J., McCluskey, G., Riddell, S., Lovett, H. (1996) *Learning to Listen*, Brookes

Lovett, H. (1996) *Learning to Listen: positive approaches and people with difficult behaviour,* Jessica Kingsley, London.

Luckner, J. Schauermann, D. and Allen, R. (1994) *Learning to be a Friend,* Perspectives on Deafness, vol.12 no.5. pp. 2-7.

Ludlum, C. (2002) *One Candle Power- Seven Principles that enhance lives of People with Disabilities and Their Communities,* Inclusion Press, Toronto.

Mahaffey, H. (2005) *Good Practice Guide*, Hammersmith and Fulham LEA

Maines and Robinson (1982) *No Blame Approach*, Lucky Duck

Mallory, B. and New, R. (1994) *Social Constructivist Theory and Principles of Inclusion: Challenges for Early Childhood Special Education,* Journal of Special Education vol. 28, no. 3, pp. 322-337.

Mason, M. and Rieser, R. (1992) *Disability Equality in the Classroom-A Human Rights Issue,* Disability Equality in Education, London

Maturana (1985) *The mind is not in the head*, Social Biological Structures

Masters, G. (1997) *Reintegrative Shaming in Theory and Practice,* PhD dissertation Lancaster University.

Morris, Allison and Gabrielle Maxwell. (1998) *Restorative Justice in New Zealand: Family Group Conferences as a Case Study,* Western Criminology Review 1 (1).

McCarthy, I. (ed.) (1994) Human Systems vol. 5. Nos 3-4 Special Issue: *Poverty and Social Exclusion.*

McGrath, Jim (April 2002 – 2003) Family Group Conference: Tackling Absenteeism In Southend Evaluation Report (NetCare Consultancy Ardfreelin Newry)

McKnight J. (1998) *The Careless Society*

McLeod, J. (1997) *Narrative and Psychotherapy,* Sage Publications, London

Miers, D et al (2001) *An Exploratory Evaluation of Restorative Schemes,* Crime Reduction Research Series paper 9, Research, Development and Statistics Directorate, 2001.

Merton, Robert K. (1968) *Social Theory and Social Structure,* Free Press, p. 477

Milton Keynes Educational Psychology Service, 2006. Restorative Group Conferences in Milton Keynes Schools. Milton Keynes Council. Incentive Plus.

Morrison, B.E. (2001) *The school system: Developing its capacity in the regulation of a civil society,* in J. Braithwaite & H. Strang (eds.), Restorative Justice and Civil Society, Cambridge University Press, Cambridge, pp. 195–210.

Morrison, Brenda (2001) http://www.realjustice.org/library/morrison_bullying.html

Mosely, J. (1990) *The Circle Book*, Positive Press. Trowbridge Wilts.

Mosely, J. (1996) *Quality Circle Time in the Primary Classroom,* LDA.

New Local Government Network, (June, 2007) *Reducing Reoffending*

Newton, C. and Wilson, D. (2005) *Creating Circles of Friends,* Inclusive Solutions

Newton, C. and Wilson, D. (2006) *Circles of Adults,* Inclusive Solutions

OFSTED (2005). The 2005 OfSTED Report *Managing Challenging Behaviour*

Oliver, C. (2005) Reflexive inquiry *A framework for consultancy practice* p.3 Karnac

Olweus, D. (1993) *Bullying at School,* Blackwell Publishers.

Olweus, D. (1994) *Annotation: Bullying at School: Basic Facts and Effects of a School based Intervention Program,* Journal of Child Psychology and Psychiatry, 35, pp.117-90.

O'Brien J. and O'Brien C. L. (2002) *Implementing Person centered Planning',* Inclusion Press. Toronto

O'Connor, Paddy: Principal, Letterkenny, Vocational School, Ireland, (2004) *Restorative Justice at work in Letterkenny Vocational School*

Owen, Harrison (2003) *Open Space Technology*

Pearpoint, J.(2002) *Hints for Graphic Facilitators,* Inclusion Press, Toronto

Pearpoint, J. Forest, M. and Snow, J.(1993) *The Inclusion Papers- Strategies to Make Inclusion Work,* Inclusion Press, Toronto.

Passmore, B. (2003) Times Educational Supplement 13th December 2003.

Pearce, W.B. (1995) *An introduction to systemic therapy with individuals,* Fran Hedges

Pearce, W.B. (1995) *A Sailing Guide for Social Constructionists,* in Leeds-Hurwitz, W.(ed) Social Approaches to Communication New York: Guildford.

Pollard, Sir Charles (2006) Comments at '3rd International Winchester Conference'

The Prince's Trust (2002) *The Effectiveness of Peer Support Systems in Challenging School Bullying: The Perspectives and Experiences of Teachers and Pupils,* London

Quinton, D. (1987) *The Consequences of Care: Adult outcomes From Institutional Rearing,* Maladjustment and Therapeutic Education Vol. 5, No. 2 pp.18-29.

Reed, J. (2003) *Aspire to Exclude Exclusion,* Article in Times Educational Supplement 9th May 2003.

Rigby, K (1996) *Bullying in Schools and What to do about it,* Melbourne: Australian council for Education and Research.

Ritchie, J. & O'Connell, T. (2001) *Restorative justice and the contest between the relational and institutional paradigms,* in J. Braithwaite & H. Strang (eds.), Restorative Justice and Civil Society, Cambridge University Press, Cambridge, pp. 149–64.

Rogers, B. (2004) *How to Manage Children's Behaviour,* Sage

Rumi, J. (13th Century Poet) http://peacefulrivers.homestead.com/Rumipoetry1.html#anchor_13840

Sampson, E. E. (1993) *Celebrating the other: A dialogic account of human nature,* London, Harvester Wheatsheaf

Sampson, R. and Laub, J.H. (1993) *Crime in the Making: Pathways and Turning Points through Life,* Cambridge, MA: Harvard University Press.

Sharp, S. & Smith P.K. (1994) *Tackling bullying in your school. A Practical handbook for Teachers,* Routledge

Shevin, M. *Communication Ally* in O'Brien J. and O'Brien C. L. (2002) *Implementing Person centered Planning,* Inclusion Press. Toronto

Sibbet, D. (1981) *I See What You Mean! - Empowering through Visual Language,* available via www.grove.com

Snow, J. (1994) *What's Really Worth Doing and How to do It,* Inclusion Press, Toronto. Sonneman, M. (1997) *Beyond Words – A Guide to Drawing Out Ideas,* Ten Speed Press, California

Stead, J. and Weedon, E. (2005) Universities of Edinburgh and Glasgow, Scotland Paper from *The Next Step: Developing Restorative Communities,* the IIRP's 7th_ International Conference on Conferencing, Circles and other Restorative Practices,_9-11 November 2005, Manchester, England, UK.

Strang, H. and Sherman, L.W. (2007) *Finding the best way forward: implementing restorative justice in the UK.* The Smith Institute

Sullivan, K. (1998) *The Anti-Bullying Handbook,* OUP 2000 Naylor P and Cowie H

Thorsbourne, Margaret (2002) *Restorative Practices – Schools,* Incentive Publishing

Tickell, S. and Akester, K.(2004) *Restorative Justice. "The way ahead"* p 84-89. Justice publication.

Tinker, R. (2005) *Restorative Justice Handbook,* Nottingham City/Inclusive Solutions

Thorsborne, M. & Vinegrad, D. (2002) *Restorative Practices in Schools Rethinking Behaviour Management,* Incentive Publishing.

Tonry, M. (1999) *Rethinking Unthinkable Punishment Policies in America,* UCLA Law Review,46:4.

Tutu, D. (1999) *No Future Without Forgiveness,* London: Rider.

Van Ness, D. (1986) *Crime and it's Victims: What Can We Do?* , Downers Grove, Ill. Intervarsity Press

Vygotsky, L.S. (1986) *Thought and language* (trans.newly revised by Alex Kozulin)Cambridge, Massachusettes: MIT Press (originally published in 1934).

Webster-Stratton, C. (1999) *How to promote children's social and emotional competence.* p215. PCP Publishing.

Webster-Stratton, C. (1984) *Randomised trial of two parent-training programs for families with conduct-disordered children,* Journal of Consulting and Clinical Psychology, 52 (4), 666-78. 1985,1989, 1998)

Webster-Stratton, C. (1985) *Predictors of Treatment outcome in parent training for conduct problem children,* Behavior Therapy, 16,223-43.

Webster-Stratton, C. (1989) *Systematic comparison of consumer satisfaction of three cost-effective parent training programs for conduct problem children,* Behavior Therapy, 20, 103-15.

Webster-Stratton, C. (1998) *Preventing conduct problems in Head Start children: strengthening parent competencies,* journal of Consulting and Clinical Psychology, 66,715-30.

Webster-Stratton, C. (1999) *How to promote children's social and emotional competence.* London: Paul Chapman.

Wertheimer, A. (1995) *Circles of Support- Building Inclusive Communities,* Circles Network. Bristol.
Wheatley, Margaret (2005) *Finding our Way,* BK Publishers

White, M. (1995) *Re-Authoring Lives: Interviews & Essays Adelaide,* Dulwich Centre Publications.

White, M. (1993) *Developing self esteem,* in Bovair, K. and McLaughlin, C. (Eds) Counselling in Schools - A Reader. David Fulton Publishers.

White, M. and Epston, D.(1990) *Narrative Means to Therapeutic Ends,* W.W. Norton. New York.

Webster-Stratton, C. (1999) *How to promote children's social and emotional competence*, p215. PCP Publishing.

Young, I. M. (1990) *Justice and the politics of difference,* Princeton, N.J., Princeton University Press.

Youth Justice Board, Partners in Evaluation (2005) Restorative Justice in Schools. *Summary of the national evaluation of the Restorative Justice in Schools Programme* Youth Justice Board publication

Zehr, H. (2002) *The Little Book of Restorative Justice,* Intercourse, PA: Good Books.

DVD/Video Material

Introducing Restorative Justice in action Commissioned by Milton Keynes Psychological Service (2006), produced by Living Archive. This DVD demonstrates the value of this constructive approach in resolving conflicts and repairing damaged relationships in the school community. It has a particular relevance for:

Bullying
Low-level disruption
Fighting
Serious behaviour incidents
Relationship issues.   Available from Inclusive Solutions.

Rediscovering MAPS - Charting Your Journey. Created by Jack Pearpoint, Marsha Forest and John O'Brien. A step by step guide to one form of person centred planning involving facilitation and graphic processes called MAPS. The DVD/Video provides detailed footage of the process in action with two different families. Available from Inclusive Solutions.

A *Circles of Friends* DVD is now available showing recent circles in action. This resource brings to life Circles of Friends in a fresh and appealing way. Available from Inclusive Solutions.

A *Restorative Justice at Ryton Park* DVD is also available showing the process via video footage with KS1 pupils, to support an understanding of the process. Ideal for training or preparation of a staff team prior to working with them. Available from Inclusive Solutions.

A range of inclusive resources such as DVDs and publications can be obtained via Inclusive Solutions, 49 Northcliffe Ave, Mapperley, Nottingham, NG3 6DA. Tel. 0115 9567305 www.inclusive-solutions.com

Web Sites

We have referenced a number of web sites in this book and group them here under the headings that they relate to. Some of these Web site addresses will change but hopefully may be located by searching with the additional information provided.

Anger Management

www.indiana.edu/~safeschl/AngerManagement.pdf
This pdf downloadable document describes anger management techniques. In anger management, students are taught strategies (e.g., problem-solving skills) that enable them to control their anger in the face of a conflict. Although specific elements used in anger management vary, most programs use a combination of techniques.

Assertive Discipline

www.adprima.com/assertive.htm
Behavioural Perspectives are well reflected in the Assertive Discipline Approach described on this web site. Assertive discipline in some form is likely the most widely used discipline plan in schools. Teachers who use assertive discipline say they like it because it is easy to use and is generally effective.

Bullying

www.realjustice.org/library/morrison_bullying.html Morrison, Brenda (2001)
This is a useful Australian web site that details international interventions around bullying. 'Restorative justice processes offer us an opportunity to get off the seesaw between punitive and moralistic approaches to addressing school bullying. Advocates of punitive approaches call for responsibility and accountability for behavior. Advocates of the libertarian approaches call for further care and support of the person. A restorative process involves both these components…'

www.dfes.gov.uk/bullying/
This is the UK Government's on-line version of "Don't Suffer in Silence". 'Bullying hurts and you don't have to endure it. If you are on the receiving end of bullying, there are many things that can be done to make your life easier. This web site is intended to show pupils, their families and teachers how to tackle a problem that has gone on for far too long. It is packed with new ideas, practical techniques and the valuable experiences of those who have been bullied, or have even bullied others, to demonstrate that you need not Suffer in Silence.'

Circle of Courage

www.augie.edu/dept/nast/Projects/doc6.htm
Refined over thousands of years, Native Americans' approach to child rearing challenged the narrow perspectives of many latter-day psychological theories and politicians' Zero-tolerance, get tough rhetoric. From Native American cultures, the insight of early youth work pioneers, and contemporary research, one may deduce what can be done to reclaim troubled and troubling youth. See also the work of Richard Villa at: **www.coe.wayne. edu:16080/wholeschooling/WS/WSPress/The%20Future%20of%20Education.pdf**

Circle of Friends

www.inclusive-solutions.com/circlesoffriends.asp

Circle of Friends is a restorative approach to enhancing the inclusion, in a mainstream setting, of any young person who is experiencing difficulties in school because of disability, personal crisis or because of their challenging behaviour towards others. The 'circle of friends' approach works by mobilising the young person's peers to provide support and engage in problem solving with the person in difficulty.

Emotional Literacy and fostering an emotionally literate environment.

Two websites that give a grounded account of these processes in action are:
www.creative-corner.co.uk/schools/tuckswood (a First School) and
www.westborough.kirklees.sch.uk (a High School).
See also: **www.antidote.org.uk** – resources relating to an emotional literacy audit.
www.nelig.com is the UK national emotional literacy interest group that disseminates good practice.

Evaluation Work

From 2001- 2004 a national evaluation was carried out by the Youth Justice Board across the pilot projects of the UK. The full report 'National Evaluation of the Restorative Justice in Schools Programme' (2004) can be viewed at:
www.yjb.gov.uk/Publications/Scripts/prodView.asp?idProduct=207&eP=

Externalising

www.dulwichcentre.com.au/externalising.htm Carey, Maggie and Russell, Shona (2007) 'Externalising' is a concept that was first introduced to the field of family therapy in the early 1980s. Initially developed from work with children, externalising has to some extent always been associated with good humour and playfulness (as well as thoughtful and careful practice). There are many ways of understanding externalising, but perhaps it is best summed up in the phrase, 'the person is not the problem, the problem is the problem'. The authors of this site have tried here to respond to some of the questions they are most commonly asked in training contexts about this concept.

Graphic Facilitation

www.grove.com
Sibbet, D. (1981) "I See What You Mean! - Empowering through Visual Language".

Inclusive Education

www.inclusive-solutions.com
Inclusive Solutions are a team of psychologists, trainers and consultants who with a great team of associates specialise in making inclusion a reality.
This web site is a great place to being finding practical resources to support the inclusion of children and young people however challenging or different they are.
The site also will support work on relationships, behaviour and restorative practice and is full of practical information and downloads on processes such as Circle of Friends, Circle of Adults and Community Circles. You will also find a number of links here to national and international sites supporting inclusion and restorative practices.

Peer Support

http://peersupport.ukobservatory.com/psia/PDF/spotlight%20briefing%20november %2004.pdf
This site describes peer support; clarifies principles of good practice; identifies the benefits of peer support for children, young people and the wider society; and identifies the contribution it makes to national and local education, health and social priorities. It is

for all those interested in peer support including policy makers, parliamentarians, senior management teams and youth officers.

Poetry

There is a community of the spirit.
Join it, and feel the delight
of walking in the noisy street
and being the noise.
Drink all your passion,
and be a disgrace.
Close both eyes
to see with the other eye.

http://peacefulrivers.homestead.com/Rumipoetry1.html - anchor_13840
Rumi, J. (13th Century Poet)

Protective Behaviours

www.protectivebehaviours.com
This site is about teaching young people to keep safe, work that sits alongside Restorative Justice extremely well.

Rewards?

www.alfiekohn.org/teaching/pdf/Punished by Rewards.pdf
Kohn, Alfie. (1995) 'Punished by Rewards?' A Conversation with Alfie Kohn is well documented here.
'A number of people seem to think if we call it "consequences" or insert the modifier "logical," then it's okay. "Logical consequences" is an example of what I call "punishment lite," a kinder, gentler way of doing things to children instead of working with them. Rewards and punishments are both ways of manipulating behavior. They are two forms of doing things to students. And to that extent, all of the research that says it's counterproductive to say to students, "Do this or here is what I'm going to do to you," also applies to saying, "Do this and you'll get that." Ed Deci and Rich Ryan at the University of Rochester are right when they call rewards "control through seduction." '

Restorative Justice in Scotland

www.betterbehaviourscotland.gov.uk/initiatives/piloting/accessforall/fife1.aspx
Better Behaviour Scotland web site. Ciesla, M., Fife Council Education Service, (2006)
'Restorative Approaches are being developed within a range of initiatives in Fife, Scotland all driving towards the same end – the creation of a restorative ethos in their schools. This site describes the work being undertaken.'

www.betterbehaviourscotland.gov.uk/initiatives/piloting/default.aspx
Restorative Justice in Scottish schools is well documented on this site.

www.betterbehaviourscotland.gov.uk/initiatives/piloting/accessforall/tain.aspx
McKinlay, A. (2006) Royal Academy

Restorative Justice web sites

www.transformingconflict.org is an excellent site developing restorative justice around the UK. This is the National Centre for Restorative Justice in Youth Settings:
'In a restorative environment everyone, young and old, is accountable for the impact of

their actions on others. Accountability means being able to take responsibility for those actions, being prepared to apologize and make amends and learning from the situation to do things differently another time. The emphasis is on repairing the harm done and re-building relationships so that effective teaching and learning can continue.'

www.bcrjp.org/forms.html provides some very practical school based resources and documents for free download.

www.sentienttimes.com/07/07_feb_mar/justice.html Cornwall, Pip. (2007) 'The relationship between men and women is the foundation of society. As relationships become more egalitarian, restoring and revitalizing our sense of self and increasing our ability to deeply value each other, we can turn our attention towards restoring and revitalizing communities as well.'

Systemic Approaches to Change

www.users.globalnet.co.uk/~ebdstudy/strategy/ecosys.htm is a useful source of further information on the systemic approach to school change with suggestions for further reading.

www.users.globalnet.co.uk/~ebdstudy/strategy/ecosys.htm
'The Ecological Systems Approach is the acceptance of a new perspective on the child's behaviour and how it relates to other areas of the child's existence outside the school perspective. How many times when discussing a pupil's behaviour in class, have teachers at a parents evening heard the parents saying "well they're never like this at home" or "are you sure you've got the right child". This is due to the parents' own perspective of the child behaviour within their family "system".'

APPENDIX 1
Contract Example

Contract

Date

_____

Between

_____

Name

_____

To put things right, I agree to

_____

_____

_____

_____

Pupil   Date

_____

Facilitator(s)   Date

_____

_____

Witness to this contract   Date

_____

This contract will be reviewed

Restorative Solutions - A Guide for Pupils

School should be a positive experience where you can learn and achieve your potential.

All young people have the right to learn in a safe environment without fear of being intimidated, threatened or abused in any way and everyone has a part to play in this in ensuring this does not happen.

At times young people are prevented from learning or from feeling safe by the words or actions of others for example, by:

Bullying - hitting - name calling - teasing - assault - harassment - interpupil conflict - theft - non attendance

A new scheme is being tried out in our school. It is called mediation or restorative conferencing. This is where a member of staff brings together the young person who has been hurt and the pupil who has done the harm in a structured and safe meeting. This may sometimes also involve both sets of parents/carers. The aim is to look for positive ways forward in a way which:

Allows pupils in a SAFE environment to say what has made him/her unhappy and why.

Allows the 'wrong-doer' to see what effect his/her actions have had and give him/her the chance to put things right.

Allows school, friends and families to work together and support both pupils affected so that all concerned can continue to learn at school safely.

What happens if, for example, I'm bullied?

Go to see a teacher, head of year or head teacher and explain what has happened or what is going on.

The teacher/facilitator will talk to everyone involved to find out more.

If it is a serious matter, the families of the bully will be seen (if they agree).

A meeting (conference) will be called if both parties agree and the process will be the same as a pupil to pupil conference.

Everyone involved (including parents/carers) will be asked to come.

The meeting will be held in a quiet and safe place in school. The teacher/facilitator begins the meeting and sets out rules of the meeting i.e. how people will be talking to each other.

She/he asks everyone in turn what happened and how it made him or her feel.

Everyone present has a chance to have his or her say.

The person who has done the harm or has been unkind listens to what everyone has to say and then says what she/he will do to put things right.

The teacher facilitator sets out an agreement, or this can be done by the pupils themselves.

A contract is agreed

Everyone signs the agreement and has a copy.

Each pupil has their own contract and this is shared with appropriate members of staff.

The facilitator or coordinator will follow up that the contract has been kept.

Restorative Solutions - A Guide for Parents and Carers

This is a new initiative in some schools which aims at resolving issues of conflict and victimisation affecting pupils life at school. This approach considers the views and wishes of all those involved in a dispute or victimising incident and attempts to resolve problems in a CALM AND POSITIVE way, putting right the harm that has been done.

How it works

Each school involved in the project has a link person who is a member of staff who has been fully trained in restorative methods. Also other members of staff have been trained as facilitators.

In a dispute the trained member of staff offers those involved the chance to attend a restorative conference.

The problems that can be helped by a restorative conference include:

Bullying, name calling, assault, harassment, truancy, theft, inter pupil conflict and pupil teacher conflict.

The purpose of a restorative conference is:

To bring together in a structured and controlled meeting all those affected by a particular incident in school and discuss in a calm manner.

To look at ways to put right the harm the incident has caused.

To write an agreement (contract) of the actions that will be taken.

To be supportive of all concerned being able to continue in their school life safely.

A Restorative Conference will involve:

Prior to the conference, the problem will be referred to the link person by the school, who will discuss with another facilitator or project coordinator whether the case is suitable for a restorative conference.

If suitable, the facilitator(s) will meet individually with all those directly and indirectly involved in the incident and gather relevant information.

The date, time and place for the conference will be arranged.

The meeting is structured and there is a clear format so that it is fair and balanced.

The facilitator(s) remains neutral but runs the meeting.

Everyone will be asked in turn their thoughts and feelings about the incident and how it has affected them.

The person whose behaviour has caused the problem is given the opportunity to put it right.

An agreement/contract giving details of what will be done is drawn up. Everyone present signs this and is given a copy.

The facilitator follows up that everything that has been agreed and the contract has been undertaken.

Results

The person who has been harmed is given the chance to speak for him/herself and say how the incident has affected or harmed him/her.

The person whose behaviour has caused the problem, sees the effect of the incident and is given the chance to put things right. She/he is not seen as a bad person. It is only the specific incident, and things relating to that incident which is discussed.

Because it is generally a positive and 'healing' experience, the risk of repeating the incident is reduced. This benefits those people who are important to the pupils as well as the wider community. It breaks down barriers. Those who are involved may become initially supportive and remain in contact. The agreement is a commitment shared by all present to see that harm is put right.

Restorative Solutions - A Guide for Teachers

The restorative justice approach incorporates a range of techniques in which a number of staff have been trained. Further training will be provided throughout the year. The model adopted to date is restorative conferencing which involves a process of mediation and restoration.

What is restorative conferencing?

Restorative conferencing is a tool, which can be incorporated into a school's reward and sanctions policy, whereby the pupil who has done wrong becomes accountable to those he/she has harmed.

The aim is to facilitate communication and dialogue which restores and promotes reconciliation.

It seeks to achieve agreement and reparation through dialogue between those involved in an incident where harm has occurred. Those involved are encouraged to take part in a conference. Attendance is voluntary however.

Restorative conferencing separates the person from the wrongful act, but it is essential that she/he admits that she/he has caused harm.

When can it be used?

It can be used in place of a fixed team exclusion or permanent exclusion with clear contracts being made. It can also be used following an exclusion to resolve the issue and ensure that there is no recurrence of the incident which led to exclusion.

Examples of incidents:

Bullying, name calling, inappropriate behavior, vandalism, theft, assault, interpupil conflict, teacher - pupil conflict, non attendance.

How does it work?

There is a structured format and certain phrases and styles of language are used to help the pupil reflect on how his/her actions have impacted on others and how amends can be made.

Three main strands to conferencing are:

1. Full restorative conference

The facilitator (trained member of staff) is consulted if it is felt that a Restorative Conference could be beneficial in resolving conflict.

Relevant information is gathered and facilitator decides if a conference is appropriate. If so participants are seen by facilitator, and also parents/carers if necessary. The format of the conference is explained and date then arranged.

At the conference each person in turn is asked how he or she feels about the incident and who it affected.

Important features of restorative conference are:
The facilitator remains neutral.

The 'wrong doer' is given a chance to put things right.

An agreement is drawn up. All present to sign it and are given a copy.

Emphasis is placed on restoration and reparation.

It is seen as a positive experience.

2. A short conference can be used in less formal situations - usually two pupils & the facilitator:

Someone has admitted to causing harm.

The incident is discussed and questions asked following the format of the full conference.

It is briefer than a full conference.

Some form of reparation made.

Emphasis is on reparation and restoration.

3. In and around school:

The language of restorative conferencing can be used in many situations in and around school with a pupil whose action has impacted adversely on another. It can challenge the pupil to be aware of the effects of his or her actions on others and provide an opportunity to put things right.

The emphasis of restorative conferencing is active participation in a positive and meaningful way, which encourages pupils to take responsibility for their actions.

APPENDIX 5

Conferences with Commentary

Natalie and Tanya

A Short Conference in detail with commentary on process

A 14 year old girl Natalie had been friendly with another girl (Tanya) in her year. They "fell out" when a third girl became friendlier with Tanya. Natalie began to be on the receiving end of nasty comments about her clothes and how she looked. In many of the lessons she shared with the other girls, they started to comment on how she smelled and other pupils in the class found this funny.

Natalie began to refuse to go to school and the more she stayed off the greater the hurdle became to her returning. Her mother had to take time off work and was at risk of losing her job. Natalie felt the problem escalating in her head the longer she stayed off. The other girls were totally oblivious of the distress caused and effects of what they considered, at the time, to be "a bit of a laugh". They had no idea why Natalie had not returned to school.

In this case, there was a lot of restorative groundwork and preparation to be done with Natalie, before she felt ready to come face to face with the other girl. A crucial part of the assessment involved identifying Tanya's attitude to what had been happening and working at Natalie's pace about when she felt ready for the conference to take place. If these factors had been neglected it may have been experienced as a further abuse and violation.

The restorative groundwork had to be laid before Natalie felt ready to face the other girl Tanya. A crucial part of the assessment was to identify Tanya's attitude to what had been happening and to work at Natalie's pace when she felt ready for the conference to take place. To have failed to attend to this could have been a further abuse and violation.

Both the parents of the two girls and the girls themselves wanted to attempt to resolve things for themselves without supporters. They both felt there had been some things left unresolved which had led to Tanya's exclusion and Natalie's subsequent fear of returning to school. The school also agreed to the conflict being resolved in this way.

An adequate venue within the school was secured and drinks provided.

Setting the Tone

As far as possible get a quiet place which is less likely to be interrupted by loud air conditioners, traffic noise, construction work, or loud lessons. All of these will cause distraction.

Even in the short/mini conferences it is worth planning the room and, after welcomes, check with both participants that it is ok. Different people may have slightly different comfort/safety distance zones. Managing their initial welcome and creating the space to talk is key to the process of reconnection and reintegration. The facilitator should do this initial breaking of the ice especially if either or both pupils are feeling a bit nervous, alienated or isolated.

The facilitator starts with a brief preamble welcoming each person and orientating them the purpose of the conference. Each person will have their own style.

In this case both girls were thanked for coming and reminded about their choice to come. It was recognised that they had the intention of establishing an understanding of what had broken down between them who had been affected. They had to explore how Natalie might be enabled to come back to school and how both her and Tanya could get on with their school life in a peaceful way.

Setting the Tone (continued)

The preamble can also include a very basic reminder of how we will be running the session, that everyone will have a chance to have their say and that people may have different perspectives but want everyone to feel safe in talking about it. The hope that some agreements might be reached and a brief word about follow up might be useful to mention.

In short and full conferences a facilitator might take the decision to ask one party first - usually the "offender" in the traditional conferencing model. We believe that more flexibility may be adopted in a school setting. To give this choice to the victim may be very liberating for them. Sometimes it may be appropriate to negotiate who goes first. For example, if there is quite a complex history and if both participants are able to do this fairly. This case example demonstrates this negotiation.

The question asked at this point was: Where do we need to start and who might be best to do that? Natalie asked for Tanya to start and Tanya agreed. Tanya was asked "Can you take us back the point you felt it started, telling us step by step what happened". Tanya went on to talk about the day of the fight, which she admitted to starting with Natalie, the "big scene" it created and that it had to be broken up by a teacher. She also talked about her subsequent exclusion. *The unpicking of that incident involved asking what she was thinking/feeling as she described what happened and who had been affected.* It was important, to take her back and to check what had gone on before in order to put the incident into some context. The questions around "what were you thinking/feeling?" led her to describe how she had felt "small" because she thought Natalie was "looking down her nose at her". There was a palpable pause here and for the first time in the meeting the two girls shared eye contact. Prompted by the question, "can you say a bit more about that?" Tanya was able to reflect on the times that she had been friends with Natalie and how they had enjoyed doing things together. Tanya said she felt at a bit of a loss without her.

This was one key part of this particular conference where some of the emotions were palpable and there was a shift for Tanya. To harness this opportunity to learn involved gently drawing out the meaning of some of these emotions and how they get acted out. Allowing anger to be expressed is an important element to conferences. Holding the different emotions in the room and putting them into context may be the biggest challenge for facilitator but it is often where there are strong emotions that the most powerful learning takes place.

The next question was "who do you think has been most affected by your actions?" and it had even more poignancy for Tanya, as she was able to start thinking from Natalie's position a bit more. This was elaborated on when she asked "In what way (how) was Natalie affected?" The "who else" prompt question moved her around members of her family, herself, the time she missed from school and work she had to catch up with.

At this stage before moving on to Natalie, Tanya was asked "How do you feel **now** about all this?" As well as talking about the school work she had missed, and the "hassle" with certain teachers, she did think there were some other girls trying to stir things up but she said she didn't understand why Natalie had not been back.

Notice here that closed questions such as "were you thinking about the effect of what you did?" are not used because they invite a less helpful and detailed response. More often than not the "don't know" replies or shrugging of the shoulders responses are elicited from young people when the questions are closed. Keep questions open therefore, such as "what were you thinking at the time?" and "what do you think has happened as a result of that fight?" Open questions concerning the feelings and motivations of the young person will elicit more open responses.

Before moving onto the next stage of the conference it was important to go through this same set of questions with Natalie, who was by now looking noticeably more relaxed. It was interesting and new information (for the facilitator) that Natalie chose as her starting point. She began with her friendship with Tanya and how they had "fallen out", when a third girl came between them. Natalie said that she refused to do some of the things they were getting into and had begun to be on the receiving end of nasty comments about her clothes and how she looked. She felt angry and hurt about losing the friendship but felt she didn't want to mess up her education. The fight had had a big effect on her because she didn't think it would go that far. When she described the male teacher who stopped it both girls started to laugh and seemed to make a useful connection. In exploring how people had been affected, the conference returned to the serious impact of what had occurred and what were still concerns for Natalie.

Use of humour in a conference can be helpful and appropriate. Whilst acknowledging that laughter at the expense of someone else will not be restorative, there are many functions laughter can fulfil. These include; serving to connect people positively, breaking the tension and reducing the pain caused by anger or shame. The skill of the facilitator is to notice the type of laughter and how helpful it can be to the restorative process.

Tanya addressed Natalie directly at this stage assuring her that she had not made any subsequent threats and did not want any continuation of the problem. It was important to allow this to happen without taking control. Asking Natalie "What did you think about what had been said or do you have any questions?" invited Natalie to comment on what she had heard. She felt safe enough to ask Tanya some direct questions about the rumours that were going around that she was still after her.

Drawing it together for the next stage they were both ready to consider "What needs to happen next?" Asked "What would you like to happen?" Natalie responded that she just wanted to get back to school and not be watching over her shoulder. She didn't want any of Tanya's friends coming after her.

Tanya apologised to Natalie for starting the fight and admitted she did get "wound up" at times by other people. She said that she wanted to be able at least to say hello to her. She said she would speak to the other girls and tell them not to keep it going and that it was sorted. The other girls were totally oblivious of the distress and effect of what they considered to be "a bit of a laugh" at the time and had no idea of the reason why. It was important to revisit the issue of confidentiality and what it was ok or not ok to share.

Next Natalie was asked: "How does that sound? Is there anything more that needs to be done?" And Tanya "What else can you think of to do?"

IT IS IMPORTANT NOT TO PUT WORDS INTO THEIR MOUTHS AT THIS STAGE. THE AGREEMENTS BELONG TO THEM AND ARE FAR MORE LIKELY TO "STICK" IF THEY DO THIS.

This is where you are really drawing out the details of the agreements that are being made. You can either invite them to write their own agreements separately or together or you can do it with them.

Tanya at this stage offered to meet Natalie at the bus stop for a few mornings and walk with her to school to show to others there "was no beef".
Natalie at this point also said that she did give Tanya a disdainful look at times and that she would try not to.

Both girls read out their agreements at the end and were congratulated on what they had achieved. We discussed who it would be helpful to share the agreements with. In some cases it may also be productive to ask a question about who might help the individuals keep to their agreements, which brings forth useful adults they can identify as a resource. The other side of this of course may be, as in this case, that participants can start to consider other pupils who have had a part in keeping the conflict in place. It is helpful to ask them what they might say to a friend who is insisting they should fight or is obviously spreading a rumour. They can then begin to think about potential strategies that will help them to keep to their agreements.

An appreciative question to end this conference might have been to ask something like: "who will be most proud of what you have managed to achieve here today?"

In our follow up on this case, the parents also had a chance to feedback and Natalie's mother said:

"I wasn't sure about my daughter and the bully being in the same room, because I didn't want her upset any more than she already was. It was months before she was ready but once she confronted the person she felt much better about it. She is much stronger now. At first I wanted the child punished because she hurt my daughter but she was spoken to in a serious way and she knew I was upset and that she upset N. The meeting and the contract has worked for my daughter."

Jackie and Clive's Relationship
A Full Conference

In a co-ed school a Year 10 boy Clive could not understand what "the fuss" was about when he had been reported as "inappropriately touching" a Year 9 girl, Jackie. A male member of staff had taken Clive aside and asked "why?" Clive tried to justify his behaviour; he said the Year nine girl had been "clocking", "eyeing him up" and giving him "come on messages." The teacher's approach was to try to be very firm and clear with Clive and explicitly told him to "stop doing it to Jackie", which he agreed to. Subsequently, however, things came to a head in the dining hall during the lunch break when the Year nine girl Jackie threw her food, tray and everything within her reach over the year ten boy and had to be separated from him "kicking and punching". This caused a huge disturbance and mess and it was Jackie immediately who had to "answer for" her "disruptive" behaviour. Initially reluctant to say anything, Jackie had found the whole experience quite embarrassing and difficult to talk about, she felt no one would listen as she was seen as a bit of "a trouble maker" by some members of staff. She was "punished". Exclusion was mentioned and that possibility made her more enraged. She was subsequently "formally" disciplined and sent home with a letter to her parents.

Her parents were on the phone immediately to the school saying that their daughter had her bottom pinched, while queuing for her dinner and they were appalled at how she had been treated. Her older brother was also threatening to come to the school "to sort the boy out". This situation, responded to in the punishment frame, was quickly building momentum and was having a detrimental affect not only on the pupil involved but also on her family.

Initial information was put forward to see if this case could be dealt with restoratively. The year ten boy at that stage was cited as the "victim". However, as more details emerged about the level of "harassment" this girl had been experiencing over a period of time and the effect upon her, the picture became more complex and serious.

A full conference was called involving parents and carers of both pupils and it was agreed to use co-facilitation; having one male and one female member of staff for balance. In cases like these no matter how skilled or neutral a facilitator may be, one party may assume you are "taking sides" simply because you share the same gender, as possibly in this case, with of one of the participants.

In this conference significant details came to light. Both these pupils had been very close friends and had been in a dating relationship during the summer. The boy was able to talk about how it had "cut him up" inside and how much it had hurt him when the girl called it off quite suddenly.

The team chose to do an unscripted conference as to have followed a script could have proved too limiting in managing the multiple layers of harm/hurt on both sides. At the stage of moving towards resolution and the agreements part of the conference there were many opportunities for learning for everyone who attended including the adults. The boy's mother came with some ideas of "boys will be boys" and "that's what kids do".

These types of comments needed to be unpacked; by asking everyone in the room about their view on such stereotypical thoughts it created an active discussion or conversation between the parents about the implications of such a position. They agreed that this type of behaviour would not be acceptable, as they got older. Doing this work in the atmosphere created within the conference process encouraged a level of participation between the adults present which was more effective, with more scope for the important learning that was happening in the room to be reinforced outside. The adults had their role in helping to create a mutual dialogue between the children and it raised awareness for those pupils about giving messages and misreading these. Each set out in detail bit by bit what they would and would not do in the future.

Listening to the level of hurt and how it had effected this girl's motivation and "will" to go to school was a powerful process. Once both these pupils were heard, they were ready to move on with a greater understanding having made some sense of the sensitive and complex feelings they had experienced. They could also consider the different effects they had on the other and how that was being "acted out".

Given the nature and sensitivity of the content that this conference uncovered, it was appropriate to return to the issue of confidentiality at the end of a conference and before the pupils and their families left the room. It was important to check with them what they would say to curious peers, friends and other pupils on both sides that want to know what went on. There was some gentle questioning from the facilitator, "what are you going to say when your friends gather round you and want to know what went on?" This therefore prompted them to practice some of their strategies and set boundaries for themselves in relation to containing private matters, before they left the room.

One important area which had to be returned to was the fact that Jackie's older brother had been heard making threats to come and challenge the boy.

Whilst this is a nice example of inviting everyone in that room to share issues of safety ultimately it is the responsibility of the facilitator to ensure that anything worrying that is raised gets addressed. The adults were asked what could be done to prevent this from happening, as "we all must ensure that all pupils are safe".

This exemplifies the "ever vigilant" facilitator thinking safety first for all those involved both inside and outside the conference. Using the language "we" and "us" invites collaborative thinking around some difficult areas and uses everyone in the room as a valuable resource to help sustain children's efforts in keeping to their agreements.

Jackie and Clive were able to peacefully co exist in the school together following the conference without further incident. Whilst never again as close as they perhaps had been, valuable lessons in life and relationship had been learned and they were both able to move on with some dignity and self respect. What more could we ask?